C#

Programming

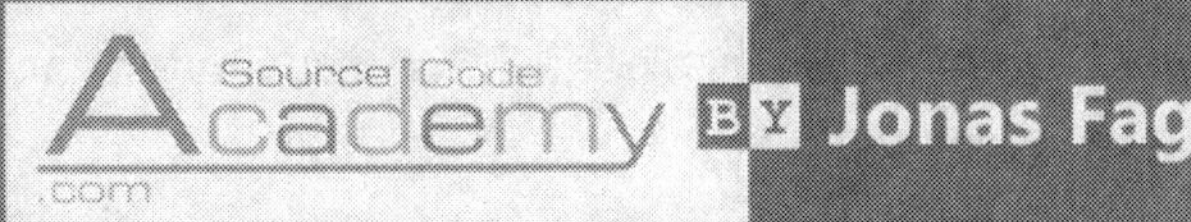

Bonus: Videos and Source Code

Speed up your learning with two free video courses and the source code from the book, available at:

Course 1: Chapter 1-9 in this book (40+ videos @ ~2h 20min)

Course 2: Unit Testing Fundamentals (6 videos @ ~1 hour)

http://sourcecodeacademy.azurewebsites.net/csharpbook.

C# Programming

You can reach the author at: info@SourceCodeAcademy.com.

ISBN: 1494208393

ISBN-13: 978-1494208394

Source code

The source code accompanying this book is shared under the MIT License and can be downloaded here:
http://www.sourcecodeacademy.com

Intended audience

This book targets beginner and intermediate developers. If the reader is a beginner programmer he/she should have some basic knowledge of programming; my recommendation is to start from the beginning of the book.

Developers with intermediate skills might want to skip the first chapters which teach basic concepts and the C# language.

This book is ideal for developers that are preparing for the MCSD Exam 70-483. The book covers the most important concepts that are needed to successfully take that exam. I suggest that the reader starts from the beginning of the book even though he/she already has the knowledge presented in those chapters. I also suggest that the reader follows the links provided in the book and searches on the internet for more information prior to taking the exam. The author and publisher give no guarantees that the reader will pass the exam.

You can find the bold text "**Additional reading:**" followed by a search term, which you can use to search for more information about the current topic. If you are reading the e-book then you can click the search term to open a browser to view the underlying web page. If a link is broken then you simply search for the search term specified.

About the author

Jonas started a company back in 1994 focusing on education in Microsoft Office and the Microsoft operating systems. While still studying at the university in 1995, he wrote his first book about Widows 95 as well as a number of course materials.

In the year 2000, after working as a Microsoft Office developer consultant for a couple of years, he wrote his second book about Visual Basic 6.0.

Between 2000 and 2004 he worked as a Microsoft instructor with two of the largest educational companies in Sweden. First teaching Visual

Basic 6.0, and when Visual Basic.NET and C# were released he started teaching these languages as well as the .NET Framework. Teaching classes on all levels for beginner to advanced developers.

From the year 2005, Jonas shifted his career towards consulting once again, working hands on with the languages and framework he taught.

This is the third book Jonas has written and it explains key concepts of C# programming for beginners to intermediate developers. He is an author with great knowledge about the C# language and the .NET framework and he has a passion for learning new things and teaching them to others. He has a knack for explaining difficult subjects in a way that is easy to understand, even for a beginner.

CONTENTS

.NET Framework & Visual Studio 2012

What is the .NET Framework?

You can use the .NET Framework 4.5 with Visual Studio 2012, a fast and efficient development platform that enables you to create applications and services. You can utilize several different solution types to create solutions for a broad range of devices.

.NET Framework consists of three main parts:

- The Common Language Runtime (CLR)
- The .NET Framework class library
- A collection of development frameworks

The Common Language Runtime (CLR)

The Common Language Runtime is a robust and highly secure execution environment that manages the execution of code. The CLR includes:

- Memory management
- Transactions
- Multithreading

The .NET Framework class library

The .NET Framework provides a class library containing common functionality and constructs that you can use when building applications. Instead of reinventing functionality you can simply reuse already existing functionality. You can also, of course, create your own class libraries that can be reused.

System.IO.File is one example of an existing class that is ready to be utilized; this particular class contains functionality to manipulate files in the Windows file system.

Development frameworks

There are several different development frameworks ready to be used when building common application types. Each framework contains the necessary components and infrastructure to get a project started.

- Windows Presentation Foundation (WPF) – Desktop applications
- XAML – Windows 8 desktop applications
- Active Server Pages (ASP.NET) Web Forms – Server-side web applications
- ASP.NET MVC – Server-side web applications
- Windows Communication Foundation (WCF) – Server-oriented web applications
- Windows Services – Long-running applications

Additional reading: "Overview of the .NET Framework"

Features

Visual Studio 2012 enables you to build applications, components and services using different programming languages and rapid design, implementation, building, testing and deployment.

Visual Studio has different views suited for different needs. You can use the *Design views* to build user interfaces, or if you want more control, you can use the *Code Editor views*. There are also wizards available for certain tasks to speed up the development.

The *Server Explorer* window enables you to log in to servers and access data and services. You can also create access and modify databases in a similar way in the Visual Studio IDE.

Visual Studio 2012 ships with a lightweight version of *Internet Information Services (IIS)* as a default web server that you can use to debug your web applications.

With the *debugging features,* you can easily follow execution paths using breakpoints and the ability to step through your code.

The *Error List* window displays errors, warnings and messages that are generated when you edit and build your code.

Coding is made more effective with *IntelliSense,* which displays a list of matching names and *code snippets* that completes the code for you by inserting it in place of a key word.

Help is always close at hand by using the integrated help feature or the online MSDN help library.

Additional reading: "What's New in Visual Studio 2013"

Templates

When starting a new project, Visual Studio 2012 makes it easy by providing templates for the most common scenarios. The templates contain starter code that you can build on when creating your application. Relevant components, controls and references to necessary assemblies for the chosen template are included from the start.

The IDE will be configured according to the template.

Console Application

The Console Application has no graphical user interface (GUI) because it is run in a Console window using a command-line interface; as such, it is considered to be very lightweight.

Windows Forms Application

Windows Forms Applications can be used to create desktop forms applications that run directly on top of the Windows operating system, not in a browser.

WPF Application

WPF is considered to be the next generation of Windows applications that gives you much more control over the user interface (UI) design. XAML is used to define the UI and C# the code behind.

Windows Store Applications

Windows Store Applications are applications that are targeted for the Windows 8 operating system. To build theses type of applications, you need skills in XAML, C#, HTML 5, CSS and JavaScript.

Class library

Building a class library will result in a .dll assembly. This is a good way to reuse code and to share it among many applications. All you need to do to reuse the .dll is reference the assembly.

ASP.NET Web Application

The ASP.NET Web Application template produces a server-side compiled ASP.NET web application that uses a browser to display the UI.

ASP.NET MVC 4 Application

The ASP.NET MVC 4 Application template produces a server-side compiled ASP.NET Model-View-Controller (MVC) application that separates the presentation (View), business logic (Controller) and data (Model) layers and uses a browser to display the UI.

WCF Service Application

The WCF Service Application template makes it possible to create Service Oriented Architecture (SOA) services.

Creating an application

When creating an application, start with one of the available project templates and modify the project to meet your requirements.

1. Open Visual Studio 2012

2. Select **File-New-Project** in the menu or use the key combination **Ctrl+Shift+N**

3. Expand the **Templates** node and the **Visual C#** node.

4. Select the appropriate template categories; for this example, choose **Windows**.

5. Select the appropriate project template from the list; for this example, choose **Console Application**.

    a. Give the project a name in the **Name** text box.

    b. Choose a folder to hold the project in the **Location** text box.

    c. Give the solution a name in the **Solution name** text box; the default name is same as the project name.

6. Click the **OK** button.

7. The **Code Editor** opens automatically and displays the default **Program** class which holds the application entry point method, **Main**.

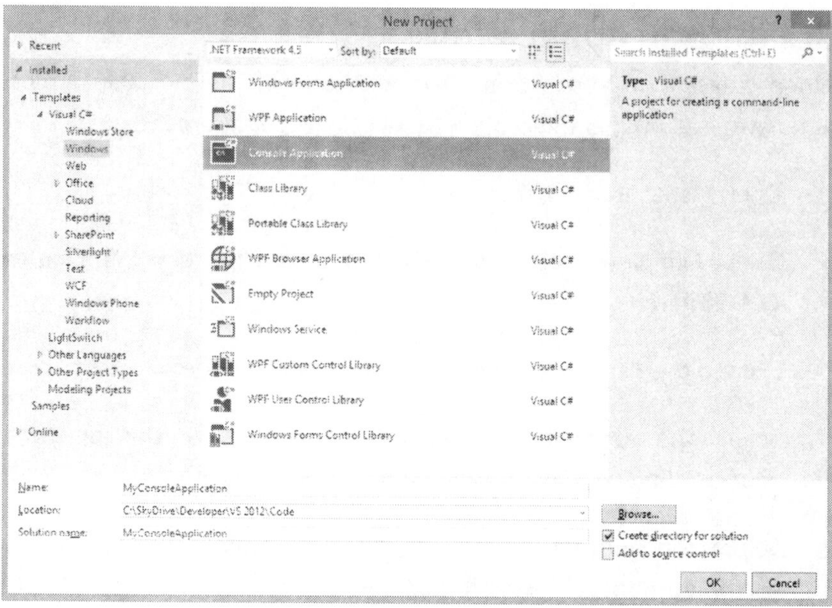

Image 1-1: The New Project dialog

The Program class

```
using System;
using System.Collections.Generic;
using System.Linq;
using System.Text;
using System.Threading.Tasks;

namespace _1_ConsoleApplication
{
    class Program
    {
        static void Main(string[] args)
        {
        }
    }
}
```

Productivity features

When coding, you get great help from the **Quick Info** functionality. **Quick Info** displays the complete declaration for any identifier in your code, just hover the mouse pointer over an identifier and the **Quick Info** will be displayed in a gray pop-up.

Image 1-2: Quick Info

When writing a variable, command or function name in the code editor, the **Complete Word** option will display a list of matches that will get progressively shorter as you type more characters. If you want to force the list to open, you can hold down the **Alt** key and press the **Right Arrow** key or you can hold down the **Ctrl** key and press the **Spacebar**.

Code snippets can make your coding more effective by inserting snippets of code when you select a snippet from the **Complete Word** list. Make sure the desired code snippet is selected and press the **Tab** key twice to insert the code.

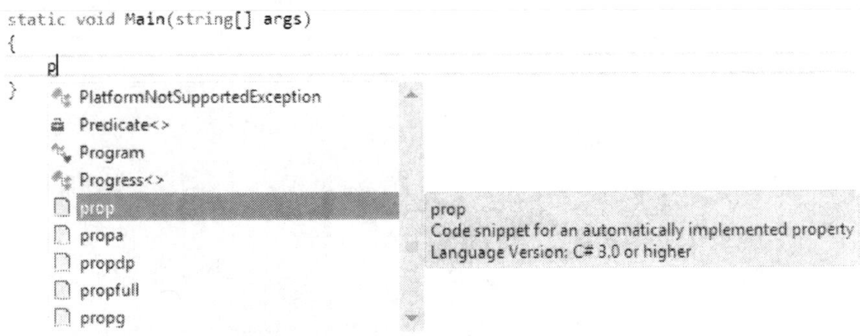

Image 1-3: Code Snippets Popup

Variables and values

All applications use data from different sources such as user interfaces, databases, network services or other sources. Variables are the way to go when storing values; operators and expressions are used to manipulate those values.

Data Types

Variables are declared as specific data types and because C# is a type-safe language, the compiler guarantees that the value stored in a variable is the correct type. The table below shows the most commonly used data types.

Type	Description	Size (bytes)	Range
Int	Whole numbers	4	-2,147,483,648 to 2,147,483,647
Long	Whole numbers	8	-9,223,372,036,854,775,808 9,223,372,036,854,775,807
Float	Floating point numbers	4	+/-3.4 x 10^38
Double	Floating point numbers	8	+/-1.7 x 10^308
Decimal	Monetary values	16	28 significant figures
Char	Single character	2	N/A

Type	Description	Size (bytes)	Range
Bool	Boolean	1	True or False
DateTime	Moments in time	8	00:00:00 01/01/0001 to 23:59:59 12/31/9999
String	Sequence of characters	2 per char.	N/A

Additional reading: "Reference Tables for Types (C# Reference)"

Expressions

An expression is made up of operands and operators. You use expressions to evaluate or manipulate data. All expressions evaluate to one value when the application runs. The result will depend on the data types and the operators that are used.

Operand

An operand is a value; it can be a number, a string or of another type. Operands can be constants (literals), variables, properties or function returns.

Operators

Operators define operations on operands. There are operators for the basic mathematical operations such as addition, multiplication, division and subtraction. There are also logical operations and operators for bit manipulation of a value.

Many of the operators in C# fall into the following categories:

1. Unary
   This type of operator is used to convert the value of a single operand and is achieved by placing the operator before the operand. One example is when you change a positive value to a negative with the minus sign (-). The positive value 1 changes to negative 1 when the – operator is placed in front of the 1; this would be the same as multiplying the value by -1.

   -1 is the same as (-1) * 1

2. Binary
   This type of operator is placed between two operands. Commonly used operations of this type are multiplying or adding values.

   2 * 3 or **3 + 4**

3. Ternary
   There is only one ternary operator in C#, **?:**. You can use this operator in conditional expressions instead of using a traditional if...then construct.

   For example
   var result = x < 11 ? 10 : 100; if **x** is less than 11 then **result** will contain 10, otherwise result will contain 100.

One important rule regarding expressions is that the type of expression must be the same as the type of the operands. This means that some operands might need to be converted to ensure compatibility.

For instance, if you divide two int values. you might expect the same result as when dividing a double with an int, but that is not the case.

Example: **5/2 = 2 (not 2.5)** and **5.0/2 = 2.5**

The following table shows the operators available in C#.

Type	Description
Arithmetic	+, -, *, /, %
Increment, decrement	++, --
Comparison	==, !=, <, >, <=, >=, is
String concatenation	+
Logical/bitwise operations	&, |, ^, !, ~, &&, ||
Indexing (counting starts from element 0)	[ ]
Casting	( ), as
Assignment	=, +=, -=, *=, /=, %=, &=, |=, ^=, <<=, >>=, ??
Bit shift	<<, >>
Type information	sizeof, typeof
Delegate concatenation and removal	+, -
Overflow exception control	checked, unchecked
Indirection and Address (unsafe code only)	*, ->, [ ], &
Conditional (ternary operator)	?:

There are classes in the .NET Framework that contains methods that you can use when performing mathematical and string operations; one of those classes is **System.Math**.

Additional reading: "C# Operators"

Using Variables

Before you can use a variable, you must declare it and give it an identifier. The identifier is the name you access the variable through. When you declare a variable, it will take up a small portion of memory to store the value associated with that variable.

You can declare multiple variables on the same line separating them with commas; all variables declared this way will have the same type.

Declaring a variable

```
int amount;
int vat;
// or
int amount, vat;
```

Assigning a variable

```
int amount;
amount = 100;
```

Declaring and assigning a variable

```
double discount = 0.5;
```

In C# you must assign a variable before using it. C# is implemented this way to avoid using variables with random values; this was a source of problems in C and C++.

Implicitly Declaring Variables

A great way to declare variables is to declare them implicitly. Instead of explicitly stating the variable type such as **int, double** or **string,** you can use the **var** keyword. The **var** keyword uses the assigned value to determine the data type. Once a value has been assigned, the data type cannot change.

In many cases, the code will be cleaner and easier to read when using the **var** keyword.

```
var discount = 0.5;
```

Additional reading: "Implicitly Typed Local Variables (C# Programming Guide)"

Object Variables

When creating a variable from a class, it is undefined before the **new** operator is used to create an object instance. The instance is placed on the heap, a memory area designated for objects. The **new** operator does two things: First, it causes the CLR to allocate memory for the object on the heap. Second, it invokes a constructor in the object to initialize its fields. A class can contain multiple overloaded constructors; which is determined by the parameters you specify when using the **new** operator.

Accessing Type Members

After an instance has been created by the new operator, you can use the variable to access the content of that object by using a period after the variable name.

When accessing a method, put a parenthesis after the method name; if the method takes parameters then pass them to the method in the parenthesis.

When accessing a property you use the property name; you can set the value if the property has a set block and get the value if it has a get block defined.

Accessing an object

```
// Create an instance
MyClass obj = new MyClass();
// Accessing the MyValue property
var value = obj.MyValue;
// Assigning a value to the MyValue property
obj.MyValue = 100;
// Calling the GetValue function that
// returns a value
value = obj.GetValue()
```

Additional reading (properties): "Properties (C# Programming Guide)"
Additional reading (methods): "Methods (C# Programming Guide)"

When a variable is delcared, it will take up a piece of memory when the application is running. Where in the memory it ends up is determined by the data type. Value type variables such as int and double will end up on the **stack** which is a fast memory storage where the values can be removed as soon as the variable goes out of scope (no longer used). Object variables on the other hand will end up on the **heap** that handles large variables. When an object variable goes out of scope, the object will undergo a clean-up process through the **Garbage Collection (GC)** which is slower that the stack.

Additional reading: "Garbage Collector Basics and Performance Hints"

Variable naming rules

There are rules for naming variables to which you must adhere.

Rule 1: An identifier can only contain letters, digits and underscore characters.

Rule 2: An identifier must start with a letter or an underscore character.

Rule 3: The identifier cannot be the same as a reserved C# keyword.

C# is case sensitive which means that you potentially could use the same variable name only changing the casing. The names *myVariable* and *MyVariable* would be two different variables. One instance when you might consider using this to your advantage is when naming a property that stores its value in a variable.

Naming variables should follow a naming convention. Use one convention and stick to it.

Casting

In an application, it is common to convert a value from one data type to another; one example is when you want to use a value from a text box, or other user interface control, and want to store the value in a variable, or use the value in a calculation.

Changing a value form one type to another is called **casting.** There are two types of casting: implicit and explicit.

Implicit Casting

Implicit conversion can be made automatically by the CLR as long as no information is lost during the cast; however, this process allows loss of precision.

Widening conversions is allowed; that is going from a smaller data type to a larger data type, for instance casting an **int** to a **long**. The other way around (**long** to **int**) is not permitted because loss of data is possible.

```
int x = 100;
long y;
y = x; // Implicit casting from int to long
```

From	To
sbyte	short, int, long, float, double, decimal
byte	short, ushort, int, uint, long, ulong, float, double, decimal
short	int, long, float, double, decimal
ushort	int, uint, long, ulong, float, double, decimal
int	long, float, double, decimal
uint	long, ulong, float, double, decimal
long, ulong	float, double, decimal
float	double
char	ushort, int, uint, long, ulong, float, double, decimal

Explicit Casting

Explicit conversions require you to explicitly write code to do the conversion. This is done when a conversion must be made and information potentially could be lost or produce an error. Beware that an explicit casting can produce an unexpected result.

This type of casting can be performed only where it makes sense, such as converting from a **long** to an **int**. You cannot use it to convert from a **string** to an **int** where the format of the data has to physically change.

```
int x;
long y = 1000;
x = (int) y; // Explicit casting from long to int
```

The System.Convert Class

You can do explicit conversions using the **System.Convert** class in cases where implicit or explicit casting isn't possible, or if you think it's easier for you to use this class for all conversions. The class contains conversion functions such as **ToDecimal**, **ToInt32** and **ToString**.

```
string myIntString = "1234";

// Conversion from string to int
int myInt = Convert.ToInt32(myIntString);
```

The TryParse Method

You can use the **TryParse** method on the data type to try and see if a conversion is possible. The function takes two parameters; the first is the value to parse and the second is a variable that will contain the parsed value if the conversion succeeds. The second parameter must be passed as an **out** parameter which means that it can pass out a value from the method.

```
string parseValue = "1234";
int parsedInt = 0;

if (int.TryParse(parseValue, out parsedInt))
{
    // On success
}
else
{
    // On failed parse
}
```

Additional reading: "Casting and Type Conversions (C# Programming Guide)"

String Manipulation

Strings are used to store alphanumerical values and can be used, for example, to store values from text boxes in a UI.

String Concatenation

You can use the **+** operator to concatenate a string, but this method of concatenation should be used sparingly because it causes overhead; every time the **+** operator is used, a new string is created in memory and the old string is discarded.

```
string myString = "first part";

myString = myString + "second part";

myString = myString + "third part";
```

You should instead use an instance of the **StringBuilder** class and append values to the instance.

```
StringBuilder mySB =
   new StringBuilder("first part");

mySB.Append("second part");
mySB.Append("third part");

string concatenatedString = mySB.ToString();
```

String Validation

String validation is very important, especially if the value comes from a UI. One way to avoid **InvalidCastExceptions** is to use regular express-ions.

The **Regex** class is located in the **System.Text.RegularExpressions** namespace. You can use the **IsMatch** method to validate if the string matches the specified criteria.

The following code validates if the string contains numerical digits.

```
var textToTest = "hell0 w0rld";
var regularExpression = "\\d";
var result = Regex.IsMatch(textToTest, regularExpression,
RegexOptions.None);
{
    // The text matched the expression.
}
```

Additional reading: "Regex Class"

The C# Language

C# provides the possibility to use conditional statements to determine the flow of an application and iterations to loop through arrays and collections of data. You can also use namespaces to structure the application and use breakpoints to debug the application.

Conditional Logic

Conditional statements are used to determine the flow of the application. For instance, you might pose a question to the user and determine the application flow based on that answer.

If

An **if**-statement is used to evaluate if a condition is **true** or **false** and, based on the result, do one of two things. An **if**-statement can be used in conjunction with an **else**-block or an **else if** statement to handle multiple scenarios.

If the condition in the **if**-statement evaluates to **true,** the **if**-block is executed; otherwise, the **else** block is executed if one exists.

If **else if**-blocks are defined then the execution will be propagated to the next **else if** statement in line until a statement evaluates to **true** or there are no more **else if** statements left.

By using a not equals (**!=**) expression you can check if the two values of a condition differ from one another. **`if(value != “some value”)`**

If statement

```
if (valueToEvaluate == true)
{
    // This code will be executed if the condition
    // evaluates to true
}
```

If...else statement

```
if (valueToEvaluate == true)
{
    // This code will be executed if the condition
    // evaluates to true
}
else
{
    // This code will be executed if the condition
    // evaluates to false
}
```

If...else if statement

```
var someValue = "Some text";

if (someValue == "Some value")
{
    // This code will be executed if the if
    // condition evaluates to true
}
else if (someValue == "Some other value")
{
    // This code will be executed if the else if
    // condition evaluates to true
}
else
{
    // Else this code will be executed
}
```

If statement inside another if statement

```
var someValue = "Some text";

if (someValue == "Some value")
{
    if (valueToEvaluate == true)
    {
    }
    else
    {
    }
}
else
{
}
```

Switch

When writing conditional statements, you should not have too many if/else clauses because it makes the code harder to read and understand; instead, you should consider using switch statements. A **switch** block is essentially a more compact and more readable way to write **if/else** clauses.

Each **case** statement ends with a **break** command. This forces the execution to jump to the end of the **switch** block. The solution will not compile if you leave out the **break** statement.

You can have a **default** block in the switch, which essentially is the same as an ending **else** clause in an **if/else** statement. This block will be executed if no **case** block is matched.

Switch

```
var valueToCheck = "The current value";

switch (valueToCheck)
{
    case "Some value":
        // Do something
        break;
    case "Some other value":
        // Do something else
        break;
    default:
        // Execute if no case is matched
        break;
}
```

Additional reading: "Selection Statements (C# Reference)"

Iterations

Iteration is a great way to execute a block of code multiple times; for instance, it can be an array or a collection of values.

For

A **for** loop is a way to iterate over a set of values until the given expression evaluates to **false**. A for loop has three parts: a start value for the loop, an expression telling the loop when to stop, and a counter.

`[int i = 0]` is the start value, `[i < 100]` is the condition that makes the loop iterate 100 times, `[i++]` is the iterator.

```
for (int i = 0; i < 100; i++)
{
    // Code to execute a hundred times
}
```

Foreach

When using a **foreach** loop, you don't have to know the number of elements that the loop will iterate over because it will iterate over all elements in an array or a collection, unless you explicitly end the loop prematurely. The following code will loop over the animals in the array.

```
string[] animals = { "cat", "dog", "bird" };

foreach (string animal in animals)
{
    // Code to execute
}
```

While

A **while** loop is a way to execute a block of code while a condition is **true**. Important to note is that a while loop will not execute if the condition is true from the beginning.

```
bool continueExecution =
CheckIfExecutionShouldContinue();

while (continueExecution)
{
    // Code to execute
    continueExecution = CheckIfExecutionShouldContinue();
}
```

The same loop could be condensed to the following code.

```
while (CheckIfExecutionShouldContinue())
{
    // Code to execute
}
```

Do

A **do** loop will, contrary to a while loop, always execute at least once.

```
bool continueExecution = true;

do
{
    // Code to execute
    continueExecution =
        CheckIfExecutionShouldContinue();
} while (continueExecution)
```

The same loop could be condensed to the following code.

```
do
{
    // Code to execute
} while (CheckIfExecutionShouldContinue());
```

Additional reading: "Iteration Statements (C# Reference)"

Arrays

An array is a sequence of values or objects that are treated as a group and managed as a unit. The most common types of arrays are one-, two- or three-dimensional (list, table and cube, respectively), but you can create arrays with up to 32 dimensions. You also can create jagged arrays. These are arrays for which you don't have to allocate memory for all elements at once, you can allocate as many as you need when you need them. Each array can have different sizes.

Creating arrays

Arrays are **zero (0) based**, meaning that the first element of an array is stored at index zero. The size of the array is determined by the number of elements you can store in it. The number of **dimensions** the array holds determines the **rank** of the array. An array always holds values or objects of the same type.

If you need to be able to store different types in the same array, consider using collections. Collections are found in the **System.Collections** namespace. Collections are expandable, which means that you can **add** and **remove objects** in the collection as needed.

An array does not allocate physical memory until the **new** operator has been executed; at this time you specify the size of the array implicitly (by assigning values directly) or explicitly (by stating the size).

When reading or writing data to an array, you should check for the **IndexOutOfRangeException** exception; this type of error will occur if you try to use an index that is not available in the array.

Declaring Arrays

```
int[] list = new int[5];
int[,] table = new int[2, 3];
int[,,] cube = new int[2, 3, 4];
string[][] jagged = new string[3][];
```

Storing Data In Arrays

```
list[0] = 10;

table[0, 0] = 1; table[0, 1] = 2; table[0, 2] = 3;
table[1, 0] = 4; table[1, 1] = 5; table[1, 2] = 6;

cube = new int[,,]
{
    {
        { 1, 2, 3, 4 }, { 5, 6, 7, 8 },
        { 9, 10, 11, 12 }
    },
    {
        { 13, 14, 15, 16 }, { 17, 18, 19, 20 },
        { 21, 22, 23, 24 }
    }
};
jagged[1] = new string[2];
jagged[1][0] = "cat";
```

```
jagged[1][1] = "dog";
jagged[2] = new string[] { "cat", "dog", "bird" };
```

Reading Data From Arrays

Reading values from an array

```
var listValue = list[0];  // returns 10
var tableValue = table[0, 1]; // returns 2
var cubeValue = cube[1, 2, 3]; // returns 24

// will return an array containing ["cat", "dog"]
var jaggedArray = jagged[1];

// will return the string "dog"
var jaggedArrayValue1 = jagged[1][1];

// will return the string "cat"
var jaggedArrayValue2 = jaggedArray[0];
```

Looping over values in an array

```
int result = 0;

for (int i = 0; i < list.Length; i++)
{
   result += list[i];
}
```

Additional reading: "Arrays (C# Programming Guide)"

Namespaces

Namespaces are used to group classes into logical **hierarchies**. In .NET Framework, there are several namespaces that group its classes logically so that you can find them easier . You can create namespaces in your application as well as to group your classes.

Namespaces also function as a **barrier** to avoid name conflicts. You cannot use the same class name more than once within a namespace, but the same name can be used if placed in different namespaces. This can be very useful if you want to use the same class name that has been used in .NET Framework, for instance.

The most important namespace is **System,** which holds classes that communicates with the operating system. Other commonly used namespaces are: **System.Windows,** which is used in UI creation, **System.IO,** which is used in file communication, **System.Data,** which is used in data access, and **System.Web,** which is used when building web applications.

User Defined Namespaces

When defining namespaces for your application, you usually start with the application-wide namespace name and add the appropriate sub-level namespaces.

Let's say you are building a bank application named *MyBank*. Your top level namespace name would most likely be *MyBank*. In this applicatio,n you will have business logic in different classes. One might be *Account* and to group these classes together, you can create a namespace for them called *Business*. To access the *Account* class, you would have to use the namespace path **MyBank.Business.Account** or use the *using* statement **MyBank.Business** to have access to the *Account* class directly.

Defining the namespace

```
namespace MyBank.Business
{
    class Account
    {
    }
}
```

Using the namespace

```
using MyBank.Business;
...
Account account = new Account();
```

Using Namespaces

If you want to access classes in a namespace, you must first import the namespace into the code file you are working in; if it's a namespace in an external class library, you must first set a reference to the appropriate assembly.

The **using** statement imports the namespace into the code file, enabling you to use its containing classes. You use the using statement to avoid having to write out the full namespace path for all usages, making the code much easier to read and maintain.

How to import an assembly

1. Right click on the **References** folder in the **Solution Explorer** window.
2. Select the appropriate assembly/assemblies (class library) from the list.
3. Click the **OK** button.

```
using System;
...
Console.WriteLine("This is a message");
```

Additional reading: "Namespace (C# Reference)"

Debugging

Debugging is one way of finding errors in the code. Being able to step through the code simplifies the task of finding out where the problem is that you need to fix. To debug an application, it must be in **Debug** mode; you can set the mode from the **Standards toolbar** located below the main menu bar.

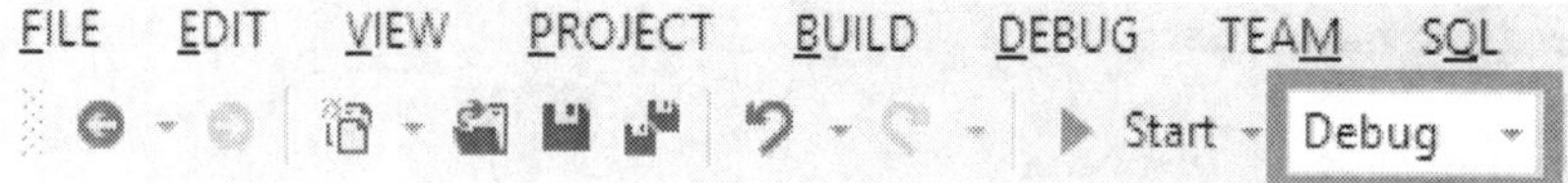

Image 3-1: Debug Setting in Main Menu

Breakpoints and windows

If you know roughly where the problem you want to debug is located, you can place a breakpoint on the row where you want to halt the execution. This enables you to use the various windows and tools available for debugging.

To set a breakpoint, click on the desired line of code and select **Toggle Breakpoint** from the **Debug menu**, press **Ctrl+F9** on keyboard, or click on the grey area to the left of the desired line of code.

To **start** the application **in debug mode,** press **F5** on the keyboard.

To check values in debug mode, you can just hover over the variable name. If you want to check or alter values, you can use one of the **Immediate**, **Autos**, **Locals** or **Watch** windows.

Debug commands

Debug menu	Button	Keyboard	Description
Start Debugging	Start/Conti nue	F5	Start application in Debug mode
Break All	Break all	Ctrl+Alt+ Break	Causes a running application to enter break mode.
Stop Debugging	Stop	Shift+F5	Stops debugging and exits the application
Restart	Restart	Ctrl+Shift+ F5	Equivalent to stop followed by start
Step Into	Step into	F11	Steps into method calls

Debug menu	Button	Keyboard	Description
Step Over	Step over	F10	Executes a method call without stepping into the code
Step Out	Step out	Shift+F11	Executes the remaining code in the current method and halts execution on the next statement in the method that made the call.

Additional reading: "Debugging in Visual Studio 2012"

Methods

It's important to divide the solution into small, logical components; methods are a way to group code into a separate piece of work. In this chapter, we will look at how to create, invoke and debug methods.

What is a Method

A **method** is a way to encapsulate operations designed for a specific purpose and to protect data that are stored in a type (a class for instance). There are many system functions that are used to run an application. One of those functions is one called Main; it defines an entry point to the application that is executed by the CLR when the application is started.

There are different types of methods, some are only used internally by the type and are not visible outside of that type, while other methods are public and available for other types to request information from an object instance of that type or that the object performs an action.

.NET Framework itself contains classes that have methods that you can use to interact with the user, computer, or the computer's operating system.

Creating Methods

All methods have two parts: a specification and a body. The **specification** defines the method name, its parameters, return type and accessibility (the scope). Each method must have a unique signature. The name and parameter list define the signature. Leaving out the accessibility will give the method private scope, making it accessible inside the type only.

Naming Methods

When naming a method, you should adhere to the same naming convention as for variables. These are best practices that you can follow.

- Use verbs or verb phrases when naming a method; it makes it easier for developers to understand the code structure.
- Use Pascal casing (each word should start with an uppercase letter); do not begin a method name with an underscore or a lowercase letter.

The Method Body

A **method body** is always enclosed in braces and is a block of code that can contain any programming construct. Variables created inside a method will go out of scope when the method ends; they can only be used inside the function.

```
void MethodWithoutParameters()
{
}
```

Parameters

All functions have a parameter list that is specified within the method parentheses; not specifying parameters leaves an empty parameter list. Each parameter is separated by a comma and is defined by a type and a name. Best practices for parameter names are to use camel case.

```
void MethodWithParameters(int positionX, int positionY)
{
}
```

Reference Parameters

When you define a reference parameter using the **ref** keyword you instruct the CLR, to pass a reference to the passed-in variable instead of passing in the value. This means that you can use the passed-in value as well as assigning a new value to that variable.

```
void MethodWithRefParameter(ref int value)
{
    value = 100;
}
```

Additional reading: "ref (C# Reference)"

Output Parameters

If you want to pass out more than a return value from a method, you can use output parameters in the parameter list. When you use output parameters, they must be assigned values within the method's body. To specify a parameter as output, you prefix it with the **out** keyword. A parameter defined as output cannot pass a value to the method, it can only pass out a value from the method.

```
void MethodWithOutputParameter(out int value)
{
    value = 200;
}
```

Additional reading: "out parameter modifier (C# Reference)"

Return Type

All methods have return types, even those that don't return a value. Use the void return type to specify that a method doesn't return a value. Methods that return a value must have a return statement in the method body. The returned value must have the same type as is used in the method declaration. When the method reaches a return statement, it ends; this means that code that occurs after the return statement will not be executed.

```
string MethodWithReturnValue()
{
    return "This is the returned string";
}
```

Calling Methods

When calling a method, you do not even have to know the inner workings of that method, you might not even have access to the code; it might be part of a third-party class library or the .NET Framework.

You call a method by specifying its name and its parameters within parentheses. If the method returns a value, you typically assign the value to a variable; if you don't need the returned value, then skip assigning it.

```
public Methods()
{
    MethodWithoutParameters();
    MethodWithParameters(10, 20);

    var value = 20;
    MethodWithRefParameter(ref value);
    MethodWithOutputParameter(out value);

    string returnedValue = MethodWithReturnValue();
    //Or
    MethodWithReturnValue();
}
```

Additional reading: "Methods (C# Programming Guide)"

Debugging Methods

Debugging is a very powerful tool when testing the application logic. When debugging methods, there are three ways to step through the code; step into, step out and step over.

Step into: Press **F11** on the keyboard to execute the statement at the current execution position; if that is a call to a function, the debugging will continue in that function. You can click the **Step into** button for the same effect; if you start the application with **Step into,** it will start in break mode.

Step over: Press **F10** on the keyboard to execute the statement at the current execution position; if that is a call to a function, the debugging will not jump into that function, but continue on the next row of code. The exception is if a breakpoint has been set in that function, then the execution will halt on that line of code.

Step out: Will execute the remaining code in the function and halt on the line of code that called the function.

Overload Methods

With overloading, you can create different implementations of methods with the same method name. Sometimes you may want to perform a task slightly different depending on the passed-in method parameters; this is when you want to use overloading. You can use the same method name for more than one method, but the signature must be different for each of the methods. The signature consists of the method name and its parameters; the parameters can be declared as output, be optional or named parameters.

Because the return type is not part of the method signature, it is not sufficient to change the return type when creating an overloaded method.

```
void OverloadedMethod()
{
}

void OverloadedMethod(int someIntValue)
{
}

void OverloadedMethod(string someStringValue)
{
}
```

```
void OverloadedMethod(string someStringValue,
int someIntValue)
{
}

string OverloadedMethod(bool someBooleanValue)
{
    return "Some string value";
}
```

Optional Parameters

One situation where you might want to use optional parameters is when interoperating with Component Object Model (COM) libraries. Since these libraries does not support overloading, you can use optional parameters instead.

Another situation you might use optional parameters in is when the compiler can't distinguish between method implementations enough to achieve overloading because the parameter list doesn't vary enough.

You declare an optional parameter by assigning it a value in the method's parameter list. All mandatory parameters must be declared before any optional parameters.

When calling a method that has optional parameters, you can omit all or some of the optional parameters; if you have more than one optional parameter and omit one, then the rest of the parameters following that parameter must be omitted as well. The method will use the default value when a parameter has been omitted.

```
void MethodWithOptionalParamters(int someIntValue,
bool optionalBoolValue = true,
bool anotherOptionalBoolValue = true)
{
}
```

```
public Methods()
{
    MethodWithOptionalParamters(10);
    MethodWithOptionalParamters(10, false);
}
```

Named arguments

Using named arguments, you can forego the order in which the parameters have been declared in a function. To use named arguments, specify the parameter name and value separated by a colon.

When used in conjunction with optional parameters, named arguments makes it easy to omit parameters. Optional parameters will receive their default values. Omitting mandatory parameters will result in a compilation error.

```
void MethodWithOptionalParamters(int someIntValue,
bool optionalBoolValue = true,
bool anotherOptionalBoolValue = true)
{
}

public Methods()
{
    MethodWithOptionalParamters(
        10, anotherOptionalBoolValue:false);
}
```

Additional reading: "Named and Optional Arguments (C# Programming Guide)"

Handling Exceptions

Exception handling is a good way to enhance the user's experience and to avoid unnecessary data loss. Errors can occur in the application logic as well as outside control of the application; for instance, you could not know if a file is accessible or that a database is online.

Checking method return values is not sufficient to catch all types of errors, mainly because not all methods return a value. It is important to know why a method failed, not only that it failed. Many errors cannot be handled by checking a return value; one such error could be running out of memory.

We use exceptions to handle all types of errors in our .NET applications. For instance, if a method tries to open a file that does not exist, an exception will be thrown. If the exception is not handled in the function, the exception will propagate to the calling function that has to be ready to handle the exception. The exception will propagate all the way to the application start-up method; if it's not handled by that method, the application will crash and a message will be displayed to the user.

In .NET Framework, all exceptions are derived from the **Exception** class. There are many specialized exceptions that can be thrown by the system, all of which have inherited the **Exception** class. You can even create your own exceptions to handle your application logic by deriving them from one of the existing exception classes.

Exception Class	Namespace	Description
Exception	System	Will handle any exception that is raised.
SystemException	System	Is the base class for all exceptions in the System namespace. Handles all errors raised by the CLR.
Application-Exception	System	Handles all non-fatal exceptions raised by the application.
NullReference-Exception	System	Handles exceptions that are related to null objects.
FileNotFound-Exception	System.IO	Handles exceptions related to missing files.

Additional reading: "Exception Class"

Try/Catch Block

Try/catch blocks are the way you implement Structured Exception Handling (SEH) in an application. To handle Exceptions that might arise, you wrap the code in a **try**-block and handle the exceptions in one or more **catch** blocks. It is recommended that you add exception handling for the general **Exception** class as the last exception-block in the catch list; this is used to handle any exceptions that you might have overlooked.

In the following code sample, the **DivideByZeroException** will be thrown when the two values are divided. The execution will recognize that an exception has occurred and execute the code in the catch block handling that exception.

```
try
{
    int result, value1 = 100, value2 = 0;
    result = value1 / value2;
}
catch (DivideByZeroException ex)
{
    // This catch block will be executed when
    // dividing by zero
}
catch (Exception ex)
{
    // This catch block will be executed for
    // any other exception
}
```

Finally Block

With a **Finally** block at the end of a **Try/Catch** block, you ensure that code that needs to be executed, regardless of if an exception has been handled or not, will be executed. Typical code that you use a **Finally** block for is to make sure that a file that the application has been using is closed, or that a database connection is closed.

```
try
{
    int result, value1 = 100, value2 = 0;
    result = value1 / value2;
}
catch (DivideByZeroException ex)
{
    // This catch block will be executed when dividing by zero
}
catch (Exception ex)
{
    // This catch block will be executed for any other exception
}
finally
{
    // Code in the finally block is always executed
}
```

Additional reading: " try-catch-finally (C# Reference)"

Throwing Exceptions

To implement exception handling in your application logic, you will need to know how to throw exceptions as well as handle them. When you throw an exception, the execution of that method ends and the exception will be passed by the CLR to the first exception handler that can handle that particular exception.

Use the **throw** keyword to throw exceptions from your application logic. It's recommended that you create your own exception classes that correspond to your application logic when the system exceptions aren't a good match; consider that you might want to pass application data with the exception; to do that you need to create a new exception class that derives from an existing exception class.

In the following code sample, an **ApplicationException** is thrown in the called method. The exception is the handled in the calling method.

```
void MethodHandlingAThrownException()
{
    try
    {
        MethodThrowingAnException();
    }
    catch (ApplicationException ex)
    {
        // This catch block will be executed when
        // the function call executes
    }
    catch (Exception ex)
    {
        // This catch block will be executed for
        // any other exception
    }
}

void MethodThrowingAnException()
{
    throw new ApplicationException(
        "This exception was deliberately thrown!");
}
```

You can re-throw an exception if the exception handler can't resolve the problem.

```
void MethodHandlingARethrownException()
{
    try
    {
        MethodRethrowingAnException();
    }
    catch (ApplicationException ex)
    {
        // This catch block will be executed
        // when the function call executes
    }
```

```
    catch (Exception ex)
    {
        // This catch block will be executed for
        // any other exception
    }
}

void MethodRethrowingAnException()
{
    try
    {
        throw new ApplicationException(
            "This exception was deliberately thrown!");
    }
    catch (Exception ex)
    {
        // Throws the exception up the call chain
        throw;
    }
}
```

Application Monitoring

As a developer in a real-world scenario, you will likely find yourself using a significant amount of time solving bugs, troubleshooting problems and optimizing the code performance. Visual Studio and .NET Framework contain several tools that can be of immense help in these situations in your daily work.

Logging and Tracing

Logging is used to write information to different logs such as a text file or the Windows event log. The type of information saved to a log is typically information about what the code is doing, such as exception information. This provides developers, users or administrators with more information when solving the underlying problem.

Tracing, on the other hand, is used when you implement your code to see what is happening; write code that that outputs information to a trace listener. The default listener is the **Output** window in Visual

Studio. The most common information to output is variable values or condition results; it helps you to figure out why the application behaves in a certain way. It is also possible to halt the application execution if you define conditions that the application can respond to; this is typically done by using an **Assert** method.

Writing to Windows Event Log

Writing information to the Windows event log is a very common task in an application. One of the overloaded static methods used when writing to the log is **EventLog.WriteEntry** which you find in the **System. Diagnostics.EventLog** class. The following three pieces of information are obligatory when writing to the log.

You open the Windows event log by navigating to the **Control Panel-Administrative Tools-Event Viewer**.

Information type	Description
The *event log*	The name of the Windows event log; this will often be the **Application** log.
The *event source*	The event source identifies where the event originated from; this is typically the application name. The event source is associated with an event log when created.
The *message*	The text you want to add to the log.

Other properties that can be used with the **EventLog.WriteEntry** are: category, event Id and event severity.

Writing to the event log requires a high level of permissions. If the application has insufficient permissions, a **SystemException** will be thrown when the application tries to use the event log.

```
public ApplicationMonitoring()
{
   WritingToTheWindowsEventLog("Application",
       "SourceCodeAcademy.com - Logging Demo",
       "Logging Demo message");
}

void WritingToTheWindowsEventLog(string eventLog,
string eventSource, string eventMessage)
{
   // Create the event source if it doesn't exist.
   if (!EventLog.SourceExists(eventSource))
       EventLog.CreateEventSource(eventSource, eventLog);

   // Log the message.
   EventLog.WriteEntry(eventSource, eventMessage);
}
```

Additional reading: "How to write to an event log by using Visual C#"

Debugging and Tracing

If you want to monitor the execution of you application, you can use the **Debug** and the **Trace** classes which are located in the **System.Diagnostics** namespace. The main difference between the two classes is that the **Debug** class is available in debug mode only, while the **Trace** class is available in both debug and release mode.

Both classes write to the **Output** window by default, but you can configure them to write to any listener. It is also possible to set up conditions that have to be met for a message to be written to the **Output** window. It is also possible to indent the output in the **Output** window to make it easier to read the result.

Two functions that you will use frequently when tracing information are **WriteLine** and **Assert**. **WriteLine** will write a line of text to the **Output** window while **Assert** is used to test a condition and interrupts the execution if the condition is not met; an error dialog box is displayed where you can choose to abort or continue the execution.

Debug

```
void DebugToTheOutputWindow()
{
    int number;
    Console.WriteLine(
        "Please type a number, and then press Enter");
    string userInput = Console.ReadLine();

    Debug.Assert(int.TryParse(userInput, out number),
        string.Format("Unable to parse {0} as integer",
        userInput));

    Debug.WriteLine(String.Format(
        "The current value of userInput is: {0}",
        userInput));

    Debug.WriteLine(String.Format(
        "The current value of number is: {0}", number));
}
```

Trace

```
void TraceToTheOutputWindow()
{
    int number;
    Console.WriteLine(
        "Please type a number, and then press Enter");
    string userInput = Console.ReadLine();

    Trace.Assert(int.TryParse(userInput, out number),
        string.Format("Unable to parse {0} as integer",
        userInput));

    Trace.WriteLine(String.Format(
        "The current value of userInput is: {0}",
        userInput));
    Trace.WriteLine(String.Format(
        "The current value of number is: {0}", number));
}
```

Additional reading: "How to trace and debug in Visual C#"

Application Profiling

Application profiling is a way to make sure that you code runs efficiently; it makes it possible to measure things like processor, memory, disk, and network usage. Visual Studio Profiling Tools are a way to analyze your applications performance.

When starting a performance session you choose what you want to sample function CPU usage, memory allocation, concurrency information (for multi-threaded applications), or detailed information about function calls. The most common starting point is function CPU usage.

Running an analysis has three steps:

1. Creating and running a performance session
   This can be done with the Performance Wizard which you can start by selecting **Analyze-Launch Performance Wizard** in the main menu. You run your application as you usually would when the session has been started; then you use parts of the application that you suspect cause the problem.

2. Analyze the profiling report
   Visual Studio will display a profiling report once you exit the application. The report contains information about things such as:

   - How much CPU time functions consume
   - A timeline that displays what the application did when
   - Warnings and suggestions on code improvement

3. Revise the code and repeat the analysis
   Fix the issues that were reported in the analysis and run a new analysis session and go through the performance report. You can compare two reports to see the changes using the Visual Studio Profiling Tools.

Additional reading: "Analyzing Application Performance by Using Profiling Tools"

Performance Counters

Performance counters are a way to collect information about and troubleshoot performance problems in your application. The counters are divided in three main groups:

- Operating system and hardware platform counters
  Make it possible to monitor processor, memory, disk, and network usage.

- .NET Framework counters
  Make it possible to monitor application statistics such as number of exceptions thrown, locks and thread usage, and monitor the garbage collector.

- Custom counters that you define
  Make it possible to monitor the application behavior; this could be the number of times a method gets called or an exception gets thrown. You only have to create a custom counter once, not every time you run the application; this is typically done in an installation routine.

Using Performance Counters

When implementing performance counters in the application, use the **PerformanceCounter** and **PerformanceCounterCategory** classes. You must use the **PerformanceCounterType** enumeration to specify a base counter when creating a custom counter. Performance counters are divided into categories for easier access; one example is the **PhysicalDisk** category that typically handles data about reading and writing to a disk.

The following code shows how to create a custom performance counter.

```
void CreateAPerformanceCounter()
{
    if (!PerformanceCounterCategory.Exists(
        "SourceCodeAcademy"))
    {
        CounterCreationDataCollection counters =
            new CounterCreationDataCollection();

        CounterCreationData noOfOrders =
            new CounterCreationData();

        noOfOrders.CounterName =
            "Calls to AddOrder function";
        noOfOrders.CounterHelp =
            "Number of orders placed";
        noOfOrders.CounterType =
            PerformanceCounterType.NumberOfItems32;
        counters.Add(noOfOrders);

        PerformanceCounterCategory.Create(
            "SourceCodeAcademy",
            "Demo a custom category",
            PerformanceCounterCategoryType
                .SingleInstance, counters);
    }
}
```

The following code shows how to increment the value of a custom performance counter.

```
PerformanceCounter counterOrders = null;

public ApplicationMonitoring()
{
    counterOrders = new
        PerformanceCounter("SourceCodeAcademy",
        "Calls to AddOrder function", false);
    AddOrder();
}
```

```
void AddOrder()
{
    // Increment the number of orders
    counterOrders.Increment();
}
```

Typically you monitor and capture data for the performance counters from the **Performance Monitor** window that can be opened from **Control Panel-Administrative Tools-Performance Monitor**. Here you can get graphical display of the counters as well as collecting data for reporting and analysis.

You find the performance counters in the **Server Explorer** window by expanding the **Servers** node, the **computer name** and then **Performance Counters**.

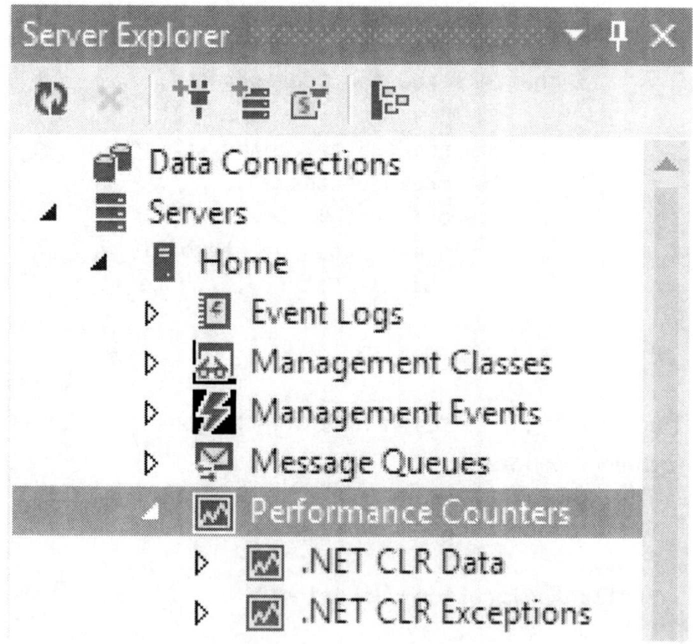

Image 4-1: Performance Counters in Server Explorer

Simple Types

You can use structs and enums to create custom simple types.

Enums

If you want to create a variable with a fixed set of values, for instance the names of the weekdays or the months; an **enum** is a good choice.

Although you theoretically could use text or numerical variables to achieve a similar result, it is not advisable. The code would be much harder to maintain. There are several benefits to using **enums**:

- Improved manageability
  It is less likely that you will run into invalid arguments and miss-pelled names using an **enum**. An e**num** restricts what values can be used because it has a fixed set of values.

- Improved developer experience
  Available values in an **enum** will be displayed with IntelliSense.

- Improved code readability
  Using an **enum** makes the code easier to read and understand.

- Improved reusability
  You can easily reuse the same **enum** in different scenarios.

Each enum member has a name and a value; the name is the string you list in the braces and the value is a zero-based integer; the first member would get the value 0, the next value 1 and so on. In our next example, Sunday would have the value 0 and Monday the value 1.

If you need to, you can assign custom values to the **enum** members by simply assigning them integer values. When using an **enum,** you can either use its integer value by casting the variable to an integer **(int)day**, or you can use the name by using the variable without casting **day**.

To use an **enum,** you create an instance variable to hold the selected value and assign a value to it by using the **enum** name and the desired value. You also can use **enums** as parameters to functions.

```
enum Weekday { Sunday, Monday, Tuesday, Wednesday,
Thursday, Friday, Saturday }

void MethodUsingEnum(Weekday day)
{
    Weekday anotherDay = Weekday.Monday;
    Debug.WriteLine(String.Format(
        "Current day is {0}: {1}", day, (int)day));
    Debug.WriteLine(String.Format(
        "Another day is {0}: {1}", anotherDay,
        (int)anotherDay));

    string result = day == anotherDay ?
        "the same" : "different";
    bool isWeekend = day == Weekday.Saturday ||
        day == Weekday.Sunday;
    Debug.WriteLine(String.Format(
        "The two days ({0}, {1}) are {2} and it is a {3}",
        day, anotherDay, result, isWeekend ?
        "weekend" : "weekday"));

    /*  The result written to the Output window is
        Current day is Saturday: 6
        Another day is Monday: 1
        The two days (Saturday, Monday) are
        different and it is a weekend  */
}
```

Additional reading: "Enumeration Types (C# Programming Guide)"

Structs

You can use the struct keyword to create custom lightweight data structures that contain information related as a single item. An example is a **struct** named Point which contains properties for x-and y-coordinates. One might argue that you could use a class instead, and that is true, but structs are faster than classes. Most built-in types like **int**, **bool** and **long** are defined by structures.

When creating a structure, the **struct** keyword is preceded by an access modifier: **public**, **internal** or **private**.

Access modifier	Description
public	Can be accessed from any assembly.
internal (default)	The type can be accessed in the same assembly, but not from other assemblies. This access modifier is used if none is specified.
private	The type is accessible only to code within the same structure or class. This requires that the type is located within another type.

You can declare constructors in a structure if you want to be able to initialize it when an instance is created. The constructor always has the same name as the structure and an empty default constructor is always created by the compiler if you don't provide a constructor in the code. It is possible to add multiple constructors to the same structure as long as they have unique sets of parameter types.

To store information in a structure, we declare fields (variables) inside the structure to hold the values. It is not recommended to use public fields in a structure; instead we use properties to get and set the private field values (see the section on Properties).

This sample shows a simple structure with a constructor.

```
public SimpleTypes()
{
    Film film = new Film(
        "Dark Shadows", "Johnny Depp", 2012);
    MethodUsingStruct(film);
}

public struct Film
{
    public string title, director;
    public int releasedInYear;

    public Film(string title, string director, int year)
    {
        this.title = title;
        this.director = director;
        this.releasedInYear = year;
    }
}

void MethodUsingStruct(Film film)
{
    Debug.WriteLine(String.Format(
        "{0} was directed by {1} and released in {2}",
        film.title, film.director, film.releasedInYear));
}

    /*  The result written to the Output window is
        Dark Shadows was directed by Johnny Depp
        and released in 2012  */
```

Properties

Properties are used for getting and setting of private field values residing in a structure or a class. One huge benefit of using properties is that you can perform data checks before setting or returning a value in property. Another benefit is that you can change the implementation of the property without impacting the client code (as long as you don't remove the property or change its access modifier or name). A third benefit is that you can bind controls to properties, but not to fields. To the consumer of the structure or the class, the property looks like a public field.

When implementing a property, we use the **get** and **set** accessors. The **get** accessor is used for returning a value from a private field using a **return** statement; the **set** accessor uses a special local variable named **value** to assign the value to the private field. The **value** variable is assigned when the client code assigns a value to the property.

You can decide how a property can be used by the client code by providing both a **get** and a **set** block (read/write), a **get** block (read only), or a **set** block (write only).

A property also can be used to assimilate data and provide the client code with a result. For instance, we could create a property that returns the full name from two private fields or properties containing the first name and last name. Or we could return or set a value based on business logic. Remember to assign values to all the private fields in the constructor.

In this sample code, we have a structure implemented with properties. The Title, Director and Year properties are read/write; the Age and **FilmInfo** properties are read only, the latter returns assimilated information from several properties and the private theatre field as a string; the Theatre property is write only. Note that we still have to assign a value to the private theatre field even though it has no value because it is passed-in through the constructor.

```
public SimpleTypes()
{
    FilmWithProperties filmWithProperties =
        new FilmWithProperties("Dark Shadows",
        "Johnny Depp", 2012, 15);

    filmWithProperties.Theatre = "The Grand Cinema";

    Debug.WriteLine(filmWithProperties.FilmInfo);
```

```
    /*  The result written to the Output window is
        Dark Shadows was directed by Johnny Depp
        and released in 2012. The film is currently
        running at The Grand Cinema.  */
}

public struct FilmWithProperties
{
    private string title, director, theatre;
    private int age, year;

    public string Title {
        get { return title; }
        set { title = value; }
    }
    public string Director {
        get { return director; }
        set { director = value; }
    }
    public int Year {
        get { return year; } set { year = value; }
    }
    public int Age { get { return age; } }
    public string Theatre { set { theatre = value; } }
    public string FilmInfo {
        get { return String.Format(
        "{0} was directed by {1} and released in {2}",
        Title, Director, Year); }
    }

    public FilmWithProperties(string title,
    string director, int year, int age)
    {
        this.title = title;
        this.director = director;
        this.year = year;
        this.age = age;
        this.theatre = String.Empty;
    }
}
```

Additional reading: "Restricting Accessor Accessibility (C# Programming Guide)"

Indexer

An indexer is a special property that makes it possible to access items in a collection within a structure or a class directly from the type name providing an integer index. This is a more intuitive way to access data instead of having to first state the array or collection name.

When creating an indexer, you use the **this** keyword that indicates that the property will be accessed through the **struct** instance name.

Let's say you have a list of films that you want to be accessible from the structure. One way would be to implement it as an ordinary array that you access with the type and array name **film.Films[0]**. The more intuitive way would be to use an indexer and access the film list from the type directly **film[0]**.

This sample code illustrates how to implement the film list scenario using a public array.

```
public SimpleTypes()
{
    FilmWithArray filmWithArray = new FilmWithArray(
        new string[] { "American Pie", "Dark Shadows",
            "We Were Soldiers" });

    Debug.WriteLine(String.Format("Selected film: {0}",
        filmWithArray.films[1]));

    /*  The result written to the Output window is
        Selected film: Dark Shadows  */
}
```

```
public struct FilmWithArray
{
    public string[] films;

    public FilmWithArray(string[] films)
    {
        this.films = films;
    }
}
```

This sample code illustrates how to implement the film list scenario using an indexer.

```
public SimpleTypes()
{
    FilmWithIndexer filmWithIndexer =
        new FilmWithIndexer(new string[]
            { "American Pie", "Dark Shadows",
            "We Were Soldiers" });
    Debug.WriteLine(String.Format("Selected film: {0}",
        filmWithIndexer[1]));
}

public struct FilmWithIndexer
{
    private string[] films;

    public string this[int index]
    {
        get { return this.films[index]; }
        set { this.films[index] = value; }
    }

    public FilmWithIndexer (string[] films)
    {
        this.films = films;
    }
}
```

Additional reading: "Using Indexers (C# Programming Guide)"

Collections

Collections is an essential tool to manage items of the same type as a set where you can add and remove items from and iterate over the items one at a time, as well as count the number of items. You can use any data type such as integers, strings and custom types such as Film with collections.

Collections are often used in graphical interfaces where they are data-bound to controls such as list boxes, drop-down lists and menus. Another neat feature is that you can use LINQ to query a collection.

Collection classes are provided by the **System.Collections** namespace.

There are several categories of collections you can use depending on the situation.

Collection type	Description
List	Store items in linear collections; you can think of a list collection as a one-dimensional array.
Dictionary	Store items using a key/value pair where each item has one key (object used to index the collection and look up the value with) and one value (the object you want to store). Example: An item could have unique film title for its key value, and the value could hold the information about that film.

Collection type	Description
Queue	Store items on a first in, first out basis; that is, the objects are read in the same order they were added. Example: This type of collection could handle added orders in turn.
Stack	Store items on a last in, first out basis; that is, the objects are read in the opposite order they were added. The item added last will be read first. Example: You could use this type of collection to determine the 20 last purchased films in a video store.

Standard Collection Classes

The following list shows the most important collection classes.

Class	Description
ArrayList	Stores objects in a linear fashion; has methods to add and remove items.
BitArray	Stores bit values as Boolean values; is most commonly used for bitwise operations and Boolean arithmetic such as AND, NOT and XOR.
Queue	Store items on a first in, first out basis; the **Enqueue** method adds an object to the back of the queue and the **Dequeue** method retrieves the item at the front of the queue.
Stack	Store items on a last in, first out basis; The Peek method makes it possible to view the topmost item without removing it, the **Push** method adds an item at the top of the stack, and the **Pop** method removes and returns the topmost item on the stack.

Class	Description
Hashtable	Is a dictionary that store items using a key/value pair; has methods to add, remove and retrieve items.
SortedList	Is a dictionary that store items using a key/value pair sorted by the key values; it has the same functionality as a Hashtable and you can retrieve values either by key or by index.

Additional reading: "System.Collections Namespace"

Specialized Collection Classes

There are specialized collections that can be used where more specialized functionality is desired.

Class	Description
ListDictionary	This collection is optimized for small amounts of data up to 10 items. If the collection will hold more data then use a HashTable.
HybridDictionary	Is a hybrid of the ListDictionary and a HashTable; using a ListDictionary when a small number of items are stored, otherwise it uses a HashTable.
OrderedDictionary	Is an indexed dictionary that lets you fetch data by key or index.
NameValue-Collection	Is an indexed dictionary where both the key and value are strings and you can fetch data by key or index.
StringCollection	This is a simple linear collection that stores strings.
StringDictionary	This is a dictionary where both the key and value are strings. You cannot use an index to retrieve

Class	Description
	values from this type of collection.
BitVector32	Is a **struct** that can represent a 32-bit value as both a bit array and an integer value; it is fixed to 32 bits and cannot be expanded and is very efficient for small values. It can be divided into sections to store multiple values in the same instance of the **struct**.

Additional reading: "System.Collections.Specialized Namespace"

Querying a collection

LINQ is a query language that can be used to query a number of data sources. LINQ is built in to .NET Languages such as Visual C# and has standardized, declarative query syntax. You can use LINQ to query data sources such as Collections, ADO.NET dataset, SQL Server databases and XML documents.

You use the following syntax when querying with LINQ:

```
from <variable names> in <data source>
group <grouping criteria>
where <selection criteria>
orderby <result ordering criteria>
select <variable name>
```

In the following example, we will fetch only the films that cost less than $10 to buy.

```
void QueryCollection()
{
    Hashtable films = new Hashtable();
    films.Add("Dark Shadows", 10.25M);
    films.Add("We Were Soldiers", 8.75M);
    films.Add("50 First Dates", 10.25M);
    films.Add("Shawshank Redemption", 9M);
    films.Add("The Dictator", 5.25M);
    films.Add("Captain America", 10.25M);

    var selectedFilms =
        from string film in films.Keys
        where (decimal)films[film] < 10.00M
        orderby films[film] ascending
        select String.Format("{0, -25}${1}",
            film, films[film]);

    foreach (string selectedFilm in selectedFilms)
        Console.WriteLine(selectedFilm);

    /*  The Dictator                $5,25
        We Were Soldiers            $8,75
        Shawshank Redemption        $9  */
}
```

There are a number of functions that you can use in conjunction with a link statement. Among them, we find **FirstOrDefault** that will fetch the first item or a default item if the collection is empty. **Max** fetches the largest item in the collection and **Min** fetches the smallest item in the collection.

In the following example, we will fetch the first and last items in the list as they have been added and sorted alphabetically. We use the list from the former example.

```
void QueryCollection()
{
    var minMaxFilms =
        from string film in films.Keys
        orderby films[film] ascending
        select String.Format("{0, -25}${1}",
            film, films[film]);

    Console.WriteLine(
        "First and last film alphabetically");
    Console.WriteLine("-------------------------------");
    Console.WriteLine(minMaxFilms.Min());
    Console.WriteLine(minMaxFilms.Max());
    Console.WriteLine();

    Console.WriteLine("First and last film");
    Console.WriteLine("-------------------------------");
    Console.WriteLine(minMaxFilms.FirstOrDefault());
    Console.WriteLine(minMaxFilms.Last());

    foreach (string selectedFilm in selectedFilms)
        Console.WriteLine(selectedFilm);

    /*  First and last film alphabetically
        -------------------------------
        50 First Dates           $10,25
        We Were Soldiers         $8,75

        First and last film
        -------------------------------
        The Dictator             $5,25
        50 First Dates           $10,25  */
}
```

Additional reading: "LINQ Query Expressions (C# Programming Guide)"

Events

Events are a way for an object to notify another object that something has happened. One type is events that are triggered by a control in a UI, such as WPF, when a user interacts with that control; it could be clicking on a button. If you write code that *subscribes* to an event, you can take some action when it is triggered.

Apart from using control events, you can create events for your types that you can *publish* to notify the application or a component as *subscribers* when something happens.

To enable other code to subscribe to an event, we create a delegate; a method signature that defines the return type and parameters for the event function it represents.

An event is associated with a delegate; you subscribe to an event by creating a method, an event handler that corresponds to the delegate and pass that method name to the *event publisher*, the object that will raise the event.

Define a delegate and an event

Suppose that you have an application that is used to sell films. It contains a Film struct that represents a film; if the film is out of stock, you need to notify the buyer that it is out of stock and maybe send an order to the ordering system to request more of that film; to accomplish this, the struct could define an OutOfStock event that the application could subscribe to.

You use the **delegate** keyword in a struct or class to define a delegate. A system delegate takes two parameters; the first is the object that raised the event and the second is the event argument, an instance of the **EventArgs** class that contains additional information that you want to pass to the subscribers.

You use the **event** keyword to define an event. It takes two parameters: the name of the delegate followed by the name that you want the event to have.

The following code sample shows how to implement the outOfStock event in the Film struct.

```
struct Film
{
    public delegate void OutOfStockHandler(Film film,
        EventArgs e);
    public event OutOfStockHandler OutOfStock;
}
```

Raising event

When a delegate and an event have been defined, you can write code to raise the event. When raising an event, all subscribers of that event will be notified and their event handler methods will be run. It's important to check if an event is null before trying to raise it because if no one is subscribing to it, it will be null and an exception will be thrown if you try to raise it. The syntax for raising an event is the same as calling a function and passing in the necessary parameters.

Suppose that the **Film struct** contain a method that checks the stock status for the film that is called every time someone tries to buy the film. We raise the **OutOfStock event** in this method if the stock level is zero; when doing so, all the subscribers will know that the film is out of stock.

The following code sample shows how to raise the OutOfStock event.

```
struct Film
{
    public delegate void OutOfStockHandler(Film film,
        EventArgs e);
    public event OutOfStockHandler OutOfStock;
    public int CurrentStockLevel { get; set; }

    private void CheckStock()
    {
        if (CurrentStockLevel == 0 && OutOfStock != null)
            OutOfStock(this, new EventArgs());
    }
}
```

Subscribing to an event

When subscribing to an event in the client code, there are two things you need to do; first, create a function that matches the event's delegate signature, and second, subscribe to the event by using the addition assignment operator (+=) to attach the client event handler method to the event. In certain cases, you only want to subscribe to an event for a while and then unsubscribe from the event. You do this by using the subtraction assignment operator (-=).

Suppose you use the Film struct in an **OrderRow** class that needs to be notified when a film is out of stock. The following code shows how you can subscribe and unsubscribe to an event.

```
class OrderRow
{
    Film film = new Film();

    private void OutOfStockHandler(Film film, EventArgs e)
    {
        // Do something when the event is raised
    }
```

```
void SubscribeToEvent()
    {
        film.OutOfStock += OutOfStockHandler;
    }

    void UnSubscribeToEvent()
    {
        film.OutOfStock -= OutOfStockHandler;
    }
}
```

Classes

Classes are a central part of object-oriented programming; a class is a construct that lets you create custom types. Classes let you encapsulate the behaviors and characteristics of logical entities. A class is like a blueprint for a type; you define the class once and can create as many object instances from it as needed; it's reusable. A class is also extendable, meaning that you can add and change the class without breaking earlier implementations; you can do this by inheritance or direct change to the class.

The characteristics and behaviors are defined by methods, fields, properties, and events.

Use the **class** keyword to create a class; although it is possible to create more than one class in a .cs file, it is recommended that you only create one class per file, unless you nest them. This makes it easier to follow the application flow.

When declaring a class, you use *access modifiers* to specify where the class can be used.

Access modifier	Description
public	The type will be accessible from any assembly, even assemblies that reference the assembly containing the type.
internal	The type is accessible from any code in the same assembly. This is the default setting if you omit the access modifier.

Access modifier	Description
private	This setting can be used only with nested types because the type will only be accessible inside the type contains it.

The class defined in this code sample is declared as public and can be used anywhere.

```
public class Order
{
    // Methods, fields, properties, and events go here
}
```

Adding Members

To define the characteristics of our Order class, we would add fields and properties; to define the behaviors we would add methods and events. The fields and properties do not have to be of reference types such as integer and decimal, they could also be defined by structs and other classes such as a collection of order rows. A behavior could be a method creating a new order or adding a new order row to the order rows collection; another behavior could be an event that is raised when a new order row has been added.

```
public class Order
{
    public int OrderId { get; set; }
    private ArrayList OrderRows = new ArrayList();

    // Define the OrderRowAdded event
    public delegate void OrderRowAddedHandler(
        OrderRow or);

    public event OrderRowAddedHandler OrderRowAdded;
```

```
public void AddOrderRow(string description)
    {
        // Create the order row
        OrderRow orderRow = new OrderRow(description);

        // Add the order row to the collection
        OrderRows.Add(orderRow);

        // Raise the event
        OrderRowAdded(orderRow);
    }
  }
```

Instantiating Classes

To use a class, you create instances of the class; instances are also called *objects*. When you create an instance of a class, two things happen; when we declare a variable using the class type, a reference pointer is created and stored using the variable name. When the **new** keyword is executed ,an object is created and memory is allocated for it.

If you like you can skip declaring what type a variable should hold and let the compiler deduce the type at compile time; you do this by using the **var** keyword when declaring a variable. Using the **var** keyword does not change how the application runs; it is only a shortcut to not having to write the type name twice.

The following code sample shows how you can create an instance of a class by using the class type or the **var** keyword.

```
public void CreateOrderRow()
{
    OrderRow OrderRow  = new OrderRow();
    // or
    var OrderRow  = new OrderRow();
}
```

When an object has been created, you can use its properties to set its values. You can also call its methods to achieve certain tasks, and subscribe to its events. You use dot notation when writing code; when you type a period after an object name IntelliSense will display a list of available members for that object.

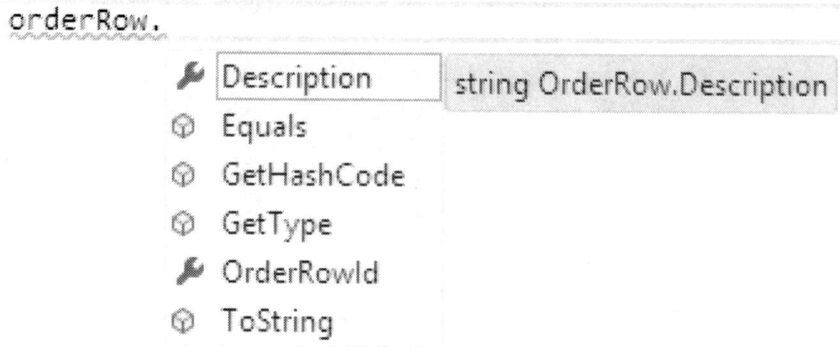

Image 8-1: IntelliSense

Constructor

A constructor is a special function that is called when an instance of a class is created. You can pass in parameters to the constructor with initial values that you use to set characteristics of the instance using its properties of fields. If no constructor is supplied in the code, a default constructor will be added by the compiler when you compile the solution.

It is possible to provide multiple constructors with different parameter lists; this is useful when you want the developer to be able to instantiate instances with different initial values, maybe a sub et of values compared with the constructor taking the most parameters.

In an order class, you could make three implementations of the constructor; one empty, one taking the description and one taking a description and an order id as parameters.

```
public class OrderRow
{
    public int OrderRowId { get; set; }
    public string Description { get; set; }
```

```
    // Instantiate with :
    // OrderRow orderRow = new OrderRow();
    public OrderRow()
    {
        OrderRowId = GetNextAvailableOrderRow();
        Description = String.Empty;
    }

    // Instantiate with : OrderRow orderRow =
    // new OrderRow("Row description");
    public OrderRow(string description)
    {
        OrderRowId = GetNextAvailableOrderRow();
        Description = description;
    }

    // Instantiate with : OrderRow orderRow =
    // new OrderRow(1001, "Row description");
    public OrderRow(int orderRowId, string description)
    {
        OrderRowId = orderRowId;
        Description = description;
    }
}
```

Reference Types vs. Value Types

There are two types of variables: value type and reference. Value types are the built-in **struct**-types such as **int**, **decimal** and **bool** as well as any **structs** you create. Value types are stored on the *stack* and are therefore much faster than reference types that reside on the *heap*. When working with a value type variable, you interact directly with its value because a value type contains its data directly.

Reference types, objects created from classes, work in a different way. A variable created from a class will not contain the data directly; instead it contains a reference (a pointer) to an allocated memory area on the *heap*. This means that before you can assign values to the variable, an instance has to be created first. Also, when the variable goes out of scope and no longer is used, the object does not simply vanish; a process called Garbage Collector will take over the reference and remove the object safely from the memory, which takes time.

If you copy an object reference to another variable, you are just creating a reference pointer to the same object; you are not creating a new instance of that type. Both variables will point to the same object in memory.

Additional reading: "Built-In Types Table (C# Reference)"

Boxing and unboxing

Boxing is the mechanism used when converting a value type to a reference type; this is useful in scenarios when a class only accepts reference types. Converting values this way is simple because you only have to assign the value type variable to the reference type variable; it is *implicit*.

```
int i = 10;
object o = i;
```

Unboxing is the mechanism used when converting a reference type variable to a value type variable; this is useful if you have a method returning or a collection storing values of the **object** data type and you need to convert it to another data type. Converting values this way requires casting from one type to another; it is *explicit*.

```
int j;
j = (int)o;
```

Static Classes

There are situations where storing instance data is unnecessary; for instance, you could create a class that contains only methods that don't store any values. It could be conversion methods or methods that return a result of some kind depending on the input parameters, such as mathematical calculations. In cases like these, a **static** class is the choice to go with; a static class cannot be instantiated and its members also need to be declared with the **static** keyword.

You access a static member through the class name.

The following code sample shows a static class with a method converting between feet and meters.

```
public static class Conversions
{
   public static decimal MetersToFeet(decimal meters)
   {
       return meters / 0.304800610M;
   }

   public static decimal FeetToMeters(decimal feet)
   {
       return feet * 0.304800610M;
   }
}

public class Test
{
   private void Convert()
   {
       decimal meters = Conversions.FeetToMeters(20);
       decimal feet = Conversions.MetersToFeet(meters);

       Console.WriteLine("meters: {0}, feet: {1}",
           meters, feet);
   }
}
```

Static Members

Static members can be useful in some circumstances such as if the functionality performed by a **static** method pertains to the type itself like keeping track of how many instances of a type have been created. No matter how many instances that are created, one instance of a static member will only ever be created.

A static member is available in all instances of a class if the class is not declared as static and contains static members. If a static property value changes, it affects all instances of that class.

A static method cannot access non-static members; this is because the static member belongs to the type and therefore have no knowledge of instances.

Unit Testing a Class

When unit testing, you should always strive to test the smallest possible unit in isolation from other things; this can be a small, self-contained class or a method in a class. A unit test has a distinct benefit; you can work with predictable and often static data sources. A good way to achieve this is to use dependency injection which means that you easily can switch to a test data source when running tests against a unit.

When writing a test function, there are three steps: First, you arrange the data, creating input values where needed and setting up the conditions for the test. Second, you act by invoking the action that you want to test; this could be creating an instance of a class and calling a function. Third, you assert the result, meaning that you verify the result from the action and failing the test if you get an unexpected result.

There are several assert functions in the **Assert** class you can use to verify the result. One that is frequently used is **Assert.IsTrue**. The assert functions may vary between different testing frameworks.

Although an application usually has a separate test project in the solution, you can create test methods in the same project; note that this is generally a bad idea because the code will be hard to follow.

To specify that a method is a test method and should be run by the testing framework, you use the **[TestMethod]** attribute with the method and the class containing the test methods must have the

[TestClass] attribute; note that the attribute may have a different name in other testing frameworks. It is important to know that you should be able to run a unit test without it breaking, even after changes have been made to the code.

In this code sample, we want to assert with unit tests that an order row collection contains order rows after the **AddOrderRow** method has been executed.

```
class ClassToTest
{
    ArrayList orderRows = new ArrayList();

    public int NumberOfOrderRows {
        get { return orderRows.Count; } }

    public void AddOrderRow()
    {
        OrderRow orderRow = new OrderRow(
            1001, "Row description");
        orderRows.Add(orderRow);
    }
}

[TestClass]
class TestingClass
{
    [TestMethod]
    public void AddOrderRow_
    NumberOfOrderRowsShouldBeGreaterThanZero_Fail()
    {
        // Arrange
        ClassToTest ctt = new ClassToTest();

        // Act
        // Here we should call the AddORderRowFunction
        // but in this scenario
        // we test to see what happens if we forget to
        // call that function.
```

```
        // Assert
        // The assert will fail because no order row
        // was added.
        Assert.IsTrue(ctt.NumberOfOrderRows > 0);
    }

    [TestMethod]
    public void AddOrderRow_
    NumberOfOrderRowsShouldBeGreaterThanZero_Pass()
    {
        // Arrange
        ClassToTest ctt = new ClassToTest();

        // Act
        ctt.AddOrderRow();

        // Assert
        // The assert will pass because an order row
        // was added.
        Assert.IsTrue(ctt.NumberOfOrderRows > 0);
    }
}
```

Interfaces

Interfaces are ways to define signatures for methods, properties, events and indexers without specifying how these members are implemented. When implementing an interface in a class, you have to implement all the members that are specified in that interface, guaranteeing the consumer that all members will be implemented. By implementing interfaces, you let the developer use a subset of the class' functionality; it is better to implement several small interfaces than one gigantic interface; remember that you have to implement all members, which can be a daunting task if you only need a small portion of the functionality.

You can implement many interfaces in one class defining different characteristics and behaviors.

Suppose that you want to implement a Movie class; you could do this by implementing an interface **IMovie** that defines what needs to be implemented in the class; for instance, release date, director, film title, and so on. Note that methods don't have any bodies in interfaces and are not declared with *access modifiers*.

Programming conventions dictate that all interface names should begin with a capital letter "I".

```
public interface IMovie
{
    string Title { get; set; }
    string Director { get; set; }
    DateTime ReleaseDate { get; set; }

    int YearsSinceRelease();
}
```

When implementing interfaces in a class you append a colon (:) to the class followed by a comma separated list with the interfaces you want to implement. When adding an interface you will be able to stub out the interface automatically by pointing to the small square at the bottom of the interface name and selecting **Implement interface** from a context menu. To implement an interface explicitly means that it is qualified by the interface it belongs to; this can make the code easier to, especially if you implement several interfaces. The only time you need to use explicit implementation is if a member with the same name and type is used in more that one of the implemented interfaces. All members will be implemented throwing a **NotImplementedException** that you remove when implementing the actual functionality of the member; it's a safety net to indicate that the members have not yet been implemented.

```
public partial class Movie : IMovie
{
}
```

Implement interface 'IMovie'

Explicitly implement interface 'IMovie'

Image 9-1: Implement Interface

```
public partial class Movie : IMovie
{
    public string Title { get; set; }
    public string Director { get; set; }
    public DateTime ReleaseDate { get; set; }
```

```
public int YearsSinceRelease()
    {
        throw new NotImplementedException();
    }
}
```

Explicit interface implementation

```
class Car : IVehicle
{
    public string IVehicle.VehicleType {
        get { return this.GetType().Name; }
    }

    public void IVehicle.Turn(int direction) { }
}
```

An interface can only have one of two *access modifiers*, either **public,** which is accessible from any assembly; or **internal**, which is accessible inside the assembly it was defined in.

An interface cannot relate to members that are internal to the class such as **fields, constants, operators and constructors**.

Interface Polymorphism

Interface polymorphism states that: *A class can be represented as an instance of any interface that it implements.* Because several classes can implement the same interface, we can use interface pointers to switch between objects at run-time depending on the application flow.

You must use explicit cast to convert from an interface type to a class type implementing the interface; this is because the class may implement other members than those defined by the interface.

```
public Polymorphism()
{
    // Representing an instance as an interface type
    Movie movie1 = new Movie();
    IMovie moveInterface1 = new Movie();

    // Casting from object to interface
    IMovie moveInterface2 = movie1;
    // Casting from an interface to a class implementing
    //the interface
    Movie movie2 = moveInterface1 as Movie;
    //or
    Movie movie3 = (Movie)moveInterface1;
}
```

Because classes that implement the same interface must implement all the members of that interface, you can use this to your advantage if you need to switch between different instances at run-time. You can use an interface pointer to hold the instance of the currently selected class type.

Suppose you are implementing an application that rents out different vehicles; when implementing the classes for car, motorcycle and scooter they all have some characteristics and behaviors that are similar; for instance, all vehicles are of a certain type and you can turn with it. You can standardize the members being implemented by using an interface called **IVehicle** that contains all the specified members and that is implemented by the classes.

The IComparable Interface

When .Net Framework collections items are sorted, for instance by calling a Sort method on the collection, they use the implementation in the **IComparable** interface. If you want collections to sort the instances of your class in a certain way, you implement the **IComparable** interface and its **CompareTo** method. The **CompareTo** method is used by the .NET Framework whenever a comparison between two instances or values is made. All the built-in types implement this interface.

The **CompareTo** method takes one argument, the object to compare the current object with, and returns an integer specifying if the current instance should be placed before, in the same position or after the passed-in object instance.

Suppose you have instances of a Book class stored in an ArrayList collection that you want to sort alphabetically by the Title property; to do this you implement the **IComparable** interface and its **CompareTo** method comparing the Title of the objects in the collection when the Sort method of the collection is called.

```
public partial class Book : IComparable
{
    public string Title { get; set; }

    public Book(string title)
    {
        Title = title;
    }

    public int CompareTo(object obj)
    {
        Book book = obj as Book;
        return String.Compare(this.Title, book.Title);
    }
}
```

The IComparer Interface

If you want to compare two objects using a custom comparer class implementation, you implement the **IComparer** interface and its **Compare** method. Using this type of implementation, you can create very sophisticated comparisons; you are also very clear what type of comparison is being used because you pass an instance of the comparer class you created to the Sort method of the collection. It is also easy to update and reuse the comparison should it be needed.

One major difference between the **IComparer** and The **IComparable** interfaces is that the **IComparer** interface is implemented in a stand-alone class whereas the **IComparable** interface is implemented in the class that is used to create collection items.

The **IComparer** Interface

```
public interface IComparer
{
    int Compare(Object x, Object y)
}
```

This code sample shows how to implement the **IComparer** Interface to compare book ratings.

```
class BookComparer : IComparer
{
    public int Compare(object x, object y)
    {
        Book book1 = x as Book;
        Book book2 = y as Book;

        return book1.Rating.CompareTo(book2.Rating);
    }
}
```

This code sample shows how to sort a collection of Book items using the custom comparer class that implements the **IComparer** Interface.

```
class IComparerImplementation
{
    public IComparerImplementation()
    {
        ArrayList books = new ArrayList();
        books.Sort(new BookComparer());
    }
}
```

Additional reading: " IComparable Interface"

Type-Safe Collections

Collections are used in almost every application that you build; in most cases, you store objects or values of the same data type in a collection. The standard collections that are available such as ArrayList and Hash-Table are not type safe and can store objects of different types.

```
public void UseStandardCollection()
{
    ArrayList books = new ArrayList();
    books.Add(new Book("Lord of the Rings"));
    books.Add(new Book("The Color of Magic"));

    // We can add instances that differ from the
    // Books type
    books.Add(new Car());

    // The run-time will throw an exception because the
    // collection contains objects of different types
    books.Sort();

    // The run-time will throw an exception because
    // you cannot cast a Car to a Book
    Book book = (Book)books[2];
}
```

In many scenarios, this can be a cause for concern because you need to do extra checks to make sure that the right type is stored in the collection; this is especially important when sorting an array because in the method used when comparing objects, casting will be done; if you store different types in the same collection, an exception can potentially be thrown.

To solve the problem with collections that are not type-safe, *generics* can be used. When you create a generic collection, the collection will be strongly typed and therefore type safe. A strongly typed collection can only store objects of one specified type. There are other benefits to using generic collections, among them are that you don't need to use casting when retrieving a values] from the collection; *boxing* and *unboxing* of value types are not necessary; not having to cast and do *boxing* and *unboxing* makes the collection much faster than a standard collection.

When creating *generic* classes, you include the **T** parameter in the class or interface; you specify the type for the **T** parameter when instantiating the class. You place the **T** parameter in angle brackets after the class name and in place of type names in the class members.

The following code sample shows how to create a *generic* class. This code is meant to show how you can use the **T** parameter in a class and its methods.

```
class GenericList<T>
{
    List<T> items = new List<T>();

    public T this[int index] {
        get { return items[index]; }
        set { items[index] = value; } }

    public void Add(T item)
    {
        items.Add(item);
    }

    public void Remove(T item)
    {
        items.Remove(item);
    }
}
```

The following code sample shows how to instantiate and use a *generic* class. Note that when we instantiate the **GenericList** class, we pass in the type in the angle brackets; by doing so, we make the collection type safe because now only books can be stored in it. This means that when calling the Add or Remove method, it automatically knows what type to expect because it uses the same *generic* type **T** as the class. Also note that on the last row of the function, we do not need to use casting, again because the collection only can contain instances of one type.

```
public void UseGenericList()
{
    GenericList<Book> gl = new GenericList<Book>();
    Book book1 = new Book("Lord of the Rings");
    Book book2 = new Book("The Color of Magic");
    gl.Add(book1);
    gl.Add(book2);
    Book firstBook = gl[0];
}
```

Constraining Generics

In certain scenarios you might want to restrict what types are allowed to be used with a generic class; the logic of you application will decide if, where and what type of restrictions are necessary.

Suppose you only want the developers using this *generic* class to be able to use it with classes that implement a certain interface then you can constrain the generic class to only accept classes that have implemented that particular interface. To constrain a generic class, you use the **where** keyword.

```
class ConstrainedClass<T> where T : IVehicle
{
    public void Drive(T item)
    {
    }
}
...
```

```
public void UseConstrainedClass()
{
    ConstrainedClass<IVehicle> cc =
        new ConstrainedClass<IVehicle>();
    cc.Drive(new Car());
    cc.Drive(new Motorcycle());

    // This row will throw a pre-compilation error
    // because Book does not implement IVehicle
    cc.Drive(new Book());
}
```

The following constraints can be applied to a *generic* class. You can apply multiple of these constraints to a single class.

Constraint	Description
where T : <name of interface>	The type argument must be, or implement, the specified interface.
where T : <name of base class>	The type argument must be, or derive from, the specified class.
where T : U	The type argument must be, or derive from, the supplied type argument U; for instance **where T : Vehicle**.
where T : new()	The type argument must have public default constructor.
where T : struct	The type argument must be a value type.
where T : class	The type argument must be a reference type.

Additional reading:

"Constraints on Type Parameters (C# Programming Guide)"

"An Introduction to C# Generics"

Generic Collections

Generics are most frequently used with **List** and **Dictionary** collections that store objects of type **T**.

Generic List Collections

This is a very powerful alternative to a non-type safe **ArrayList** collection that stores any type of objects. The **List<T>** class provides a way to create type-safe strongly typed collections; it contains functions such as Add, Remove, Insert and Sort (using the default or custom comparer).

This sample code shows how you can add, remove and sort items in a generic **List** collection.

```
void UseListCollection()
{
    List<Book> books = new List<Book>();
    books.Add(new Book("Lord of the Rings", 4.5));
    books.Add(new Book("The Color of Magic", 3.5));
    books.Add(new Book("Bilbo", 3.7));

    books.Sort();

    Book firstBook = books[0];
    books.Remove(firstBook);
}
```

Generic Dictionary Collections

This is a very powerful alternative to a non-type safe **HashTable** collection that stores any type of key-value pair. The **Dictionary<TKey, TValue>** class provides a way to create type-safe strongly typed dictionary collections; it contains functions such as **Add**, **Remove** and **OrderBy** to sort the collection using Lambda to choose what value to sort on.

Trying to add an item with a key that already exists in the collection will result in an **ArgumentException**.

This sample code shows how you can add, remove and sort items in a generic **Dictionary** collection.

```
void UseDictionaryCollection()
{
    Dictionary<string, Book> books =
        new Dictionary<string, Book>();

    books.Add("0000-0000-0000", new Book(
        "Lord of the Rings", 4.7));
    books.Add("1111-1111-1111", new Book(
        "The Color of Magic", 3.6));
    books.Add("2222-2222-2222", new Book(
        "Bilbo", 4.1));

    // Sort the collection using Lambda
    books.OrderBy(b => b.Value.Title);
    PrintCollection(books);

    // Two ways to remove the first book from the
    // collection
    KeyValuePair<string, Book> firstBook = books.First();
    books.Remove(firstBook.Key);
    books.Remove(books.First().Key);
}
```

You also can create generic list collections using **LinkedList<T>**, **Queue<T>** and **Stack<T>**; and generic dictionary collections using **SortedList<TKey, TValue>** and **SortedDictionary<TKey, TValue>**.

Collections Interfaces

In certain situations, you want to use collection interfaces; if you want to create a generic method that handles all types of collections, maybe to display values, you could pass in an **ICollection** interface to the method. Another scenario would be if you want to create your own collection class, then you most likely would implement one of the collections described in this section.

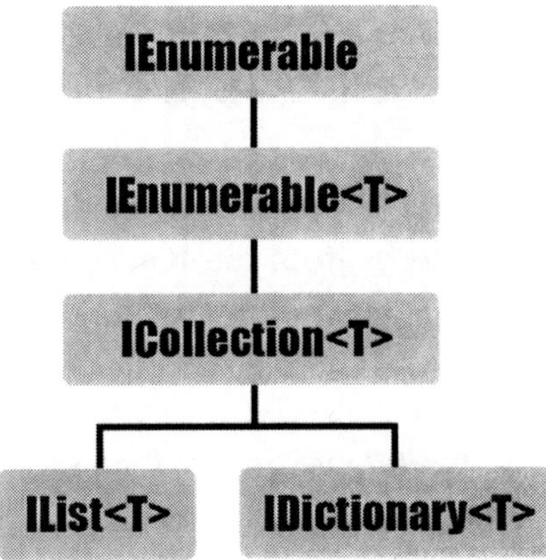

Image 10-1: Collection Interfaces

IEnumerable and IEnumerable<T>

The **IEnumerable<T>** interface inherits from the **IEnumerable** interface that implements a method called **GetEnumerator** which returns an **IEnumerator<T>** type that is used when iterating over a collection using the **foreach** statement. This means that you, for generic collections, have to implement both interfaces.

IEnumerator<T>

The **IEnumerator<T>** interface implements the functionality that all enumerators must implement; it defines the method **MoveNext** that moves the enumerator to the next item in the collection, and **Reset** moves the enumerator to its starting position, which is before the first item; it also implements the **Current** property that holds the current item.

An enumerator is essentially a pointer pointing to an item in the collect-ion.

ICollection<T>

The **ICollection<T>** interface inherits from the **IEnumerable<T>** interface, which means that you have to implement its methods. **ICollection<T>** contains the basic functionality for generic collections and defines the methods **Add, Clear, Contains, CopyTo** and **Remove**; it also defines the properties **Count** and **IsReadOnly**.

IList<T>

The **IList<T>** interface inherits from the **ICollection<T>** interface which means that you have to implement its methods. **IList <T>** can be used when creating linear collections holding single values.

IList <T> contains the basic functionality for using indexers in generic collections and defined the methods **Insert** and **RemoveAt**; it also defines the property **IndexOf**.

IDictionary<TKey, TValue>

The **IDictionary<T>** interface inherits from the **ICollection<T>** interface which means that you have to implement its methods. **IDictionary <T>** can be used when creating dictionary collections holding key-value pairs.

IDictionary <T> contains the basic functionality for generic dictionary collections and defines the methods **Add, ContainsKey, GetEnumerator, RemoveAt** and **TryGetValue**; it also defines the properties **Item, Keys** and **Values; Keys** and **Values** are collections of type **ICollection** that store the item keys and values.

The **GetEnumerator** method returns an enumerator of **KeyValuePair <TKey, TValue>** objects. The **TryGetValue** method tries to fetch a value from a key value and store it using an output parameter; the function returns true if the value is successfully fetched, otherwise it returns false and the output parameter is unchanged.

Additional reading: "System.Collections.Generic Namespace"

Create an Enumerable Collection

When creating an enumerator, you need to define what item it should treat as the first item and in what order it should move through the collection items.

The default enumerator method is **GetEnumerator,** which moves forward in the collection; it is possible to implement other enumerator methods such as **MoveBackwards**.

This code sample shows how you can implement a custom collection using the generic **IEnumerable<T>** interface and implement the additional **IEnumerator<T>** function **Reverse** that reverses the collection.

The yield **keyword** is used to indicate that the method, operator, or get accessor in which it appears is an iterator.

Additional reading: "yield (C# Reference)"

```
class MyGenericCollection<T> : IEnumerable<T>
{
    List<T> collection = new List<T>();

    public void Add(T item)
    {
        collection.Add(item);
    }

    public void AddRange(T[] items)
    {
        collection.AddRange(items);
    }

    public IEnumerator<T> Reverse()
    {
        foreach (var item in collection.Reverse<T>())
        {
            yield return item;
        }
    }
```

```
    #region Implementation of IEnumerable<T>
    public IEnumerator<T> GetEnumerator()
    {
        foreach (var item in collection)
        {
            yield return item;
        }
    }

    IEnumerator IEnumerable.GetEnumerator()
    {
        throw new NotImplementedException();
    }
    #endregion
}

class GenericCollections
{
    void UseMyGenericCollection()
    {
        MyGenericCollection<Book> books =
            new MyGenericCollection<Book>();

        books.Add(new Book("Lord of the Rings", 4.7));
        books.Add(new Book("The Color of Magic", 3.6));
        books.Add(new Book("Bilbo", 3.7));

        IEnumerable<Book> reversedBookList =
            books.Reverse<Book>();
    }
}
```

Inheritance

Inheritance is the possibility to specialize a class that already exists by reusing the already-existing class. It is a very powerful tool in your object-oriented developer's toolkit. When inheriting a class, you are reusing the characteristics and behavior of an already-existing class; then you specialize your class by adding new characteristics and behavior in the form of methods, properties and other programming constructs.

Using inheritance saves money and time by reducing the amount of code you have to write. Object hierarchies that can be used interchangeeably depending on requirements are another benefit of using inheritance.

When inheriting, you take an existing class and use it as a base class, as a source of already-implemented methods, properties and other constructs, and reuse it in your new class instead of starting from scratch.

You can only inherit from one class but implement several interfaces.

Suppose you are creating an application that deals with different types of flying machines; you could then build an inheritance chain where you start out with the most general class, FlyingMachine, that implements only what is common to all flying machines. Then you inherit the **FlyingMachine** class to more specialized classes, Plane and Saucer, which are different types of flying machines and therefore have characteristics and behaviors suited to planes and saucers. Then you decide to specialize it further to different sub-categories and the different characteristics and behaviors for each category.

In the flying machine scenario, the **FlyingMachine** class would be the base class for **Plane** and **Saucer** and those two classes respectively would be base classes for the different categories that are created. Another way of putting it is that the category classes are deriving from the **Plane** or the **Saucer** classes; and the **Plane** and **Saucer** classes are deriving from the **FlyingMachine** class.

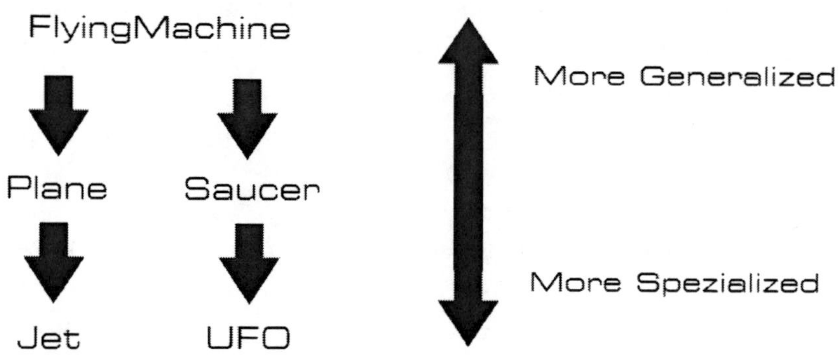

Image 11-1: Flying Machine Example

```
class FlyingMachine
{
   public void Drive() { }
   public void Stop() { }
}

class Plane : FlyingMachine
{
   public int NumberOfFloors { get; set; }
   public bool HasFirstClass { get; set; }
}
```

```
class Saucer : FlyingMachine
{
   public bool HasAlienTechnology { get; set; }
   public bool IsFromEarth { get; set; }
}

class Jet : Plane
{
   public bool IsSupersonic { get; set; }
}

class UFO : Saucer
{
   public bool HasWarpSpeed { get; set; }
}
```

The following code sample shows how to use the classes and what is available in each class. Members shown in bold are defined in that class and are not inherited.

```
Void usingTheSpecializedClasses()
{
   FlyingMachine fm = new FlyingMachine();
   fm.Drive();
   fm.Stop();

   Plane plane = new Plane();
   plane.Drive();
   plane.Stop();
   plane.HasFirstClass = true;
   plane.NumberOfFloors = 2;

   Jet jet = new Jet();
   jet.Drive();
   jet.Stop();
   jet.NumberOfFloors = 3;
   jet.HasFirstClass = true;
   jet.IsSupersonic = false;
```

```
Saucer saucer = new Saucer();
saucer.Drive();
saucer.Stop();
saucer.HasAlienTechnology = false;
saucer.IsFromEarth = true;

UFO ufo = new UFO();
ufo.Drive();
ufo.Stop();
ufo.HasAlienTechnology = true;
ufo.IsFromEarth = false;
ufo.HasWarpSpeed = true;
```

Base Classes

When working in a project, you should ask yourself if and when you or other developers need to use the class you are creating as a base class for inheritance. You have full control over how a class can be inherited if you choose to make it inheritable.

Abstract

It is not uncommon to create abstract classes that will be used only as base classes. The members of an abstract class' members do not have to have completely implemented functionality, it can even have missing functionality. It is up to you to decide if a developer can create instances of a class you are creating. If you want the class to be used in inheritance only and do not want the possibility to create instances of the class, then you add the **abstract** keyword to the class declaration.

When adding members to an abstract class, you can choose to create them with the **abstract** keyword, in which case they will be conceptually similar to interfaces in that they have to be overridden and implemented by the deriving class and no implementation is available in the **abstract** class. It is possible, however, to create fully implemented non-abstract members that can be used directly by a deriving class.

Abstract members cannot have a **private** *access modifier*.

```
abstract class MyAbstractClass
{
    internal bool NonAbstractProperty { get; set; }

    internal void NonAbstractMethod()
    {
        // Do something
    }

    internal abstract bool AbstractProperty { get; set; }

    internal abstract void AbstractMethod();
}
```

This code sample shows how to use the abstract class.

```
class DerivingFromMyAbstractClass : MyAbstractClass
{
    void UseMemebers()
    {
        NonAbstractProperty = false;
        NonAbstractMethod();

        // These members need to be overridden
        // before using them
        AbstractProperty = true;
        AbstractMethod();
    }

    internal override bool AbstractProperty { get; set; }

    internal override void AbstractMethod()
    {
        // Do something
    }
}
```

Sealed

In some circumstances, you might want to prevent developers from inheriting a class; you can accomplish this by adding the sealed keyword to the class declaration, creating an un-inheritable class.

When creating a class that derives from another class, you might want to prevent further inheritance; you can do that by adding the **sealed** keyword to your class declaration.

The **sealed** and **abstract** keywords cannot be used on the same class since they are the opposite of one another.

Static classes are sealed and cannot be inherited and **static** members in a non-static class will not be inherited.

```
// This class cannot be inherited and must be
// instantiated
sealed class MySealedClass
{
   bool MySealedClassProperty { get; set; }
}
```

Base Class Members

Declaring a member of a class with the **virtual** keyword makes it possible for developers to override or replace the member in a derived class. When overriding the method in the deriving class, you use the **override** keyword on the method.

```
class MyBaseClass
{
   public virtual void DoSomething() {
       throw new NotImplementedException();
   }
}

class MyDerivingClass : MyBaseClass
{
   public override void DoSomething() {
       // Implementation goes here
   }
}
```

New vs. Override

You also can use the **new** keyword to override a member; there is a subtle difference between the **override** and **new** keywords. The result when using the **new** keyword on a base class instance variable that is assigned an instance of a derived class might not be what you expect.

Note the output for the third scenario in this sample code in particular.

```
class BaseClass
{
   public virtual void Method1() {
Console.WriteLine("Base - Method1"); }
   public virtual void Method2() {
Console.WriteLine("Base - Method2"); }
}

class DerivedClass : BaseClass
{
   public override void Method1() {
Console.WriteLine("Derived - Method1 (override)"); }
   public new void Method2() {
Console.WriteLine("Derived - Method2 (new)"); }
}

class BaseClassMemebers
{
   private void NewVsOverride()
   {
      Console.WriteLine("BaseClass output");
      BaseClass baseClass = new BaseClass();
      baseClass.Method1();
      baseClass.Method2();
      //Output
      //Base - Method1
      //Base - Method2

      Console.WriteLine("\nDerivedClass output");
      DerivedClass derivedClass = new DerivedClass();
      derivedClass.Method1();
      derivedClass.Method2();
```

```
        //Output
        //Derived - Method1 (override)
        //Derived - Method2 (new)

        Console.WriteLine(
            "\nBaseClassAsDerivedClass output");
        BaseClass baseClassAsDerivedClass =
            new DerivedClass();
        baseClassAsDerivedClass.Method1();
        baseClassAsDerivedClass.Method2();
        //Output
        //Derived - Method1 (override)
        //Base - Method2
    }
}
```

Additional reading: "Knowing When to Use Override and New Keywords (C# Programming Guide)"

Sealing overridden members

Sealing overridden members is a way for you to force deriving classes to use your implementation. You make a member sealed by using the **sealed** keyword on methods declared using the **override** keyword. Members are by default sealed unless you declare them using the **virtual** keyword; it is only on overridden methods in derived classes that you can use the **sealed** keyword.

```
class MyBaseClass
{
    public virtual void DoSomething() {
        throw new NotImplementedException();
    }
}

class MyDerivingClass : MyBaseClass
{
    public sealed override void DoSomething() {
        // Cannot be overridden if inherited
    }
}
```

Access Modifiers

To control where a class or a member will be accessible there are five *access modifiers* that you can use. Members are **private** by default and will not be directly accessible from derived classes; to access a **private** member, you have to create a property or method to expose it.

Access modifier	Description
public	Available from any assembly
protected	Available internally in the class and in classes deriving from the class containing the member.
Internal	Available in the assembly where the class is located.
protected internal	Available in the assembly where the class is located and in classes deriving from the class containing the member.
private	Available in the class containing the member.

The following code sample is based on the Corleone family and the police interrogating them; it will shed light on the different access modifiers that can be used and their restrictions.

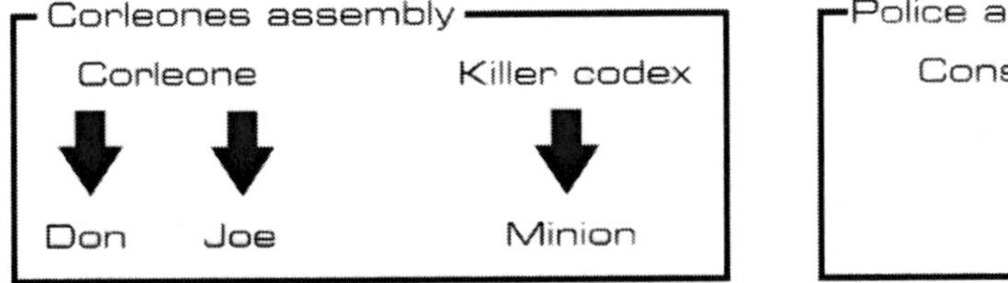

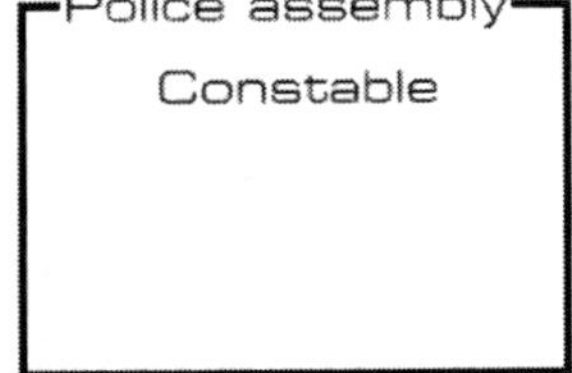

Image 11-2: Corelone and Police Assemblies

In the **Corleones** assembly, we find the classes related to the Corleone family and their minions that do the dirty work for the family. The **Corleone** class is the base class that all Corleone family members inherit from (**Don** and **Joe**). The family has a honor codex that all of their minions who aspire to be hit men have to adhere to. That codex is represented by the **KillerCodex** class; this is the base class for all minions. The **Minion** class represents one of the hit men that the family uses. Outside of the family, we have the constables who chase the family and try to catch them; the **Constable** class is located in the **Police** assembly.

The Corleone class

The Corleone class is declared as **public** which means that it can be reached from any assembly. All members are declared as internal which means that they can be reached within the Corelone assembly, but not from the Police assembly. The GetMinion and AddMinion methods are declared as **virtual** which means that they can be overridden when the **Corelone** class is inherited.

```
public class Corleone
{
    internal List<Minion> Minions = new List<Minion>();

    internal virtual Minion GetMinion(string name) {
        throw new NotImplementedException();
    }

    internal virtual void AddMinion(Minion minion) {
        Minions.Add(minion);
    }
}
```

The Don class

This class represents the father of the family and the leader of the organization. This class **inherits** the Corleone class and will have access to its members. The Don class is declared with the sealed keyword which means that it cannot be inherited.

Don Corleone has a family secret that is closely guarded and only the family knows about it; this information and the lie that he tells the police when they are pounding on the door is declared as **private** because he want the possibility to choose who will know what.

One thing that is public knowledge is that he has a son named Joe. **Joe** is declared as a separate class of which an instance is stored in the **Don** class because they have a relationship; the instance is created in the **Don** class' constructor and the **Don** instance is passed to the **Jon** instance to establish the relationship between father and son using the **this** keyword.

What Don will tell the family when they ask about the secret is represented by the **TellFamily** property that is declared as **internal** to make sure that only members of the Corleones assembly can ever find out the truth. The property **TellPolice** is declared as **public** because anyone, even members of other assemblies, is allowed to know the lie.

The GetMinion method is inherited from the Corleones class, but is overridden using the **overrides** keyword to create an alternative implementation that will be used when Don is calling for one of his minions. The method is also declared as **internal** to make sure that only members of the Corleones assembly can ask Don to call his minions.

The **SolveProblem** method is declared as **void** only, which means that it is **private.** This means that only members in the **Don** class can call it; whenever Don wants to have a problem solved, his son will take care of it.

```
Sealed public class Don : Corleone
{
    private string familySecret = "The secret is";
    private string lie = "I have no idea";
    public Joe Son { get; set; }

    public Don()
    {
        Son = new Joe(this);
    }
```

```
    internal string TellFamily {
        get { return familySecret; }
    }

    public string TellPolice { get { return lie; } }

    internal override Minion GetMinion(string name)
    {
        return (from minion in Minions
                where minion.Name == name
                select minion).SingleOrDefault();
    }

    void SolveProblem()
    {
        Son.OrderHit();
    }
}
```

The Joe class

Joe is the son of Don and helps him run the family business; the **Joe** class is declared as **public** which means that it can be reached from any assembly and has no restrictions on inheritance. Who knows, maybe he will clone himself in the future.

The **AddMinion** is inherited from the Corleone class but is overridden. it is also declared as **sealed** which means that if the Joe class is inherited, this method cannot be overridden by a deriving class; it is also declared as **internal** which means that it only can be used inside the Corleones assembly.

The **GetMinion** is inherited from the Corleone class but is overridden and declared as **internal** which means that it only can be used inside the Corleones assembly. Note that it has a different implementation than the same method in the **Don** class.

In the **OrderHit** method that is declared as internal and only available in the Corleones assembly the Kill method of the fetched minion is called.

The **AskAboutSecret** method is declared as **public,** making it possible to access it from the Police assembly or any other assembly. Note that Joe is thinking about the family secret that he has asked his father about, but saying the lie.

```
public class Joe : Corleone
{
    private Don father;
    public Joe(Don father)
    {
        this.father = father;
    }

    internal sealed override void AddMinion(
    Minion minion)
    {
        // Code to add the minion
    }

    internal override Minion GetMinion(string name)
    {
        return Minions.SingleOrDefault(
            m => m.Name == name);
    }

    internal void OrderHit()
    {
        GetMinion("Charlie").Kill("Marty");
    }

    public string AskAboutSecret()
    {
        Console.WriteLine(
            "[Joe thinking] The Secret is: {0}",
            father.TellFamily);

        return father.TellPolice;
    }
}
```

The KillerCodex class

This class contains two methods that minions who aspire to be hit men must implement or use as is. This class is declared as internal because the police cannot be aware of this contract between a minion and the Corleone family. The contract is honored by the minion class **inheriting** the KillerCodex class.

The **ChooseWeapon** method is declared as **protected** which means that it has to be inherited to be used outside of the KillerCodex class.

The Kill method is declared as protected internal which means that it can be used either by inheritance or internally in the Corleones assembly.

```
internal class KillerCodex
{
    protected void ChooseWeapon() { }
    protected internal void Kill(string name) { }
}
```

The Minion class

This class represents one of the minions working for the family and it **inherits** the KillerCodex class and its members. The Minion class is declared as internal which means that it only is accessible within the Corleones assembly and as such not available to the police assembly; this makes the minions a secret group that only the family knows about.

Note that the Kill method does not have to be implemented to be used when Joe calls the method from the OrderHit method; The Kill method can be called by Joe because it is declared as internal in the KillerCodex class.

```
internal class Minion : KillerCodex
{
    internal string Name { get; set; }

    internal Minion(string name)
    {
        Name = name;
        ChooseWeapon();
    }

    public void Talk()
    {
        Console.WriteLine("I'm not saying anything");
    }
}
```

The Constable class

The Constable class resides in a different assembly than all the other classes because it does not belong to the family; the police may be bought but that is not the same. The constable loves to interrogate people and seizes every opportunity to interrogate the Corelones.

The class contains one method that asks Don or Joe about the secret; note however that the constable does not have any knowledge of the minion. The minion class is declared as **internal,** making it impossible for other assemblies to access it; you might say that the minions hide inside the Corleone family assembly.

```
public class Constable
{
    public void Interogate(object person)
    {
        if (person is Don)
            Console.WriteLine("[Don] {0}",
                ((Don)person).TellPolice);

        if (person is Joe)
            Console.WriteLine("[Joe] {0}",
                ((Joe)person).AskAboutSecret());
```

```
            //This code will generate a pre-compile error
            //if (person is Minion)
            //    Console.WriteLine("[Minion] {0}",
                        ((Minion)person).TellPolice);
    }
}
```

The Base Keyword

In some situations, you might want to a base class method or constructor from a derived class even though you have overridden the member. To achieve this, use the **base** keyword.

You might have overridden a method in the base class or created a new function and want to call the base class method as part of your functionality; or you want to call the base class constructor when initializing the derived class. You also might want to call a base class method from a property accessor.

When instantiating a derived class, it will automatically call the base class default constructor before any of the derived class logic is executed. Sometimes you want to call an alternate constructor instead of the default base class constructor; in these situations you use the **base** keyword in the derived class' constructor declaration.

```
public class Beverage
{
    public string Name { get; set; }
    public bool IsFairTrade { get; set; }

    public Beverage()
    {
        Name = String.Empty;
        IsFairTrade = false;
    }
```

```
    public Beverage(string name, bool isFairTrade)
    {
        Name = name;
        IsFairTrade = isFairTrade;
    }

    public virtual bool GetFairTrade()
    {
        return IsFairTrade;
    }
}

public class Tea : Beverage
{
    public double Weight { get; set; }

    public Tea() { /* Is the same as Tea() : base() */ }

    public Tea(string name, bool isFairTrade,
    double weight) : base(name, isFairTrade)
    {
        // Will call the Beverage(string name,
        // bool isFairTrade) constructor before
        // executing any code in this constructor block
        Weight = weight;
    }

    public override bool GetFairTrade()
    {
        if (!base.GetFairTrade()) {
            /* Apply for fair trade status */
        }

        return base.GetFairTrade();
    }
}
```

Extending .NET Classes

When building your solution, you should always try to extend the thousands of classes that .NET Framework provides; this ensures a standardized way of writing code and reduces the amount of code needed. There will almost always be a .NET class that you can use as a foundation.

Apart from inheriting classes, you can extend types that are *sealed* by creating *extension methods*.

When it comes to inheritance, the rules that apply to custom classes apply to the .NET classes; you can inherit from types that are not **sealed** classes or **static** and you can override **virtual** members. If the type is abstract, you need to implement all abstract members of that type.

Usually the more specialized base classes are preferable to the more general classes when inheriting, but if you find that you need to implement a lot of functionality that you do not need then go for the more general base classes.

Suppose that you want to create a linear list that stores unique items. Instead of creating the list functionality from the ground up, you could inherit from the **List<T>** class and add the **RemoveDuplicates** method.

In this sample code, we will inherit from the List<T> class and add functionality to remove duplicate items. Note that we use the Sort function of the list to make it easier to remove duplicates and that the loop starts from the end of the list when removing items to ensure that the item order is intact.

To make sure that the objects are sorted correctly, you probably want to override the Equals and CompareTo methods; we will implement the

IComparable interface and call the **CompareTo** method from the Equals method when asserting if the items in the list are equal.

The UniqueList

```
class UniqueList<T> : List<T>
{
    public void RemoveDuplicates()
    {
        base.Sort();

        for (int i = this.Count - 1; i > 0; i--)
        {
            if (this[i].Equals(this[i - 1]))
            {
                this.RemoveAt(i);
            }
        }
    }
}
```

The instance class

```
public class Book : IComparable
{
    public string Title { get; set; }

    public Book(string title)
    {
        Title = title;
    }

    public int CompareTo(object obj)
    {
        Book book = obj as Book;
        return String.Compare(this.Title, book.Title);
    }
```

```
public override bool Equals(object obj)
    {
        return CompareTo(obj) == 0; // 0 => this == obj
    }
}
```

Using the UniqueList class

```
void UseUniqueList()
{
    UniqueList<Book> books = new UniqueList<Book>();
    books.Add(new Book("The Color of Magic"));
    books.Add(new Book("Lord of the Rings"));
    books.Add(new Book("The Color of Magic"));
    books.Add(new Book("Bilbo"));
    books.Add(new Book("The Color of Magic"));
    books.RemoveDuplicates();

    // Result after removing duplicate items
    // Title: Bilbo
    // Title: Lord of the Rings
    // Title: The Color of Magic
}
```

Custom Exceptions

When creating custom exceptions, you can inherit from the general base class **Exception** that resides in the **System** namespace, or you could extend one of the more specialized exception classes such as **ApplicationException**.

All exception classes ultimately derive from the **Exception** class; it has several useful properties such as **Message** that contain information about what happened, **InnerException** can identify the exception that caused the current exception; **Source** contains the item or application that caused the error; **Data** is a key-value pair collection that can store more details about the error.

You typically create custom exceptions when either there is no built-in exception classes for the error or you need an exception that corresponds to your business logic. The name of an exception class is not meant to convey the whole nature of the error; we have a message property for this purpose.

Additional reading: "System Namespace"

When creating custom exceptions, you should strive to use the inherited properties from the **Exception** class and only add your own properties when needed.

It is customary to append *Exception* to the end of the name of a custom exception.

You throw and catch custom exceptions the same way you do with system exceptions; use the **throw** keyword and create a new instance of the custom exception class with the **new** keyword passing in the necessary parameters.

The following sample code shows how to create a custom exception class that has an additional property.

```
class MyException : Exception
{
   public int MyExceptionValue { get; private set; }

   public MyException()
   {
       // Implicitly call the base constructor
       // MyException() : base()
   }
   public MyException(string message) : base(message) { }
   public MyException(string message, Exception inner) :
       base(message, inner) { }
   public MyException(string message,
   int myExceptionValue) : base(message)
   { MyExceptionValue = myExceptionValue; }
}
```

Using the custom exception class

```
void UseCustomException()
{
    try
    {
        throw new MyException("This is the message", 100);
    }

    catch (MyException ex)
    {
        Console.WriteLine(
            "Message: {0}, Custom value: {1}",
            ex.Message, ex.MyExceptionValue);

        // Output
        // Message: This is the message, Custom value: 100
    }
}
```

Inheriting From a Generic Type

When inheriting from a generic type, you can either specify types for one or more of the parameters or leave the types as generic; it is possible to mix generic type parameters with specific types. If you provide a specific type for a parameter then the parameter is strongly tied to that type when creating instances of that class and does not have to be specified.

```
class MyCustomList<T> : List<T> { }
class MyCustomList : List<int> { }
class MyCustomDictionary<TKey, TValue> : Dictionary<TKey,
TValue> { }
class MyCustomDictionary<TKey, TValue> :
Dictionary<string, TValue> { }
```

Extension Methods

Inheritance is generally used for extending classes, but in some cases such as when dealing with a sealed class inheritance is not possible. In these cases you can extend a class by using *extension methods*.

An extension method does not change the underlying type because it is a type of static method. Extension methods must be declared as **static** and the first parameter must specify the type you want to extend, you do this by placing a **this** keyword before the parameter; extension methods must be placed within a **static** class.

Extension methods are frequently used in MVC applications, for instance, to output HTML.

You must place a using statement to the extension class in the class where you intend to use the extension method.

This sample code shows how to create an extension method of the **Sytem.String** type.

```
public static class MyExtensions
{
    public static bool ContainsNumbers(this string value)
    {
        return Regex.IsMatch(value, @"\d");
    }
}
```

This sample code shows how to use an extension method.

```
void UseExtensionMethod(string str)
{
    bool hasNumbers = str.ContainsNumbers();
}
```

Reading and Writing to Files

The .NET Framework classes that handle I/O functionality are in the System.IO namespace. In this namespace, we find classes to read and write to files and manipulate files and directories; many of the methods are static, which means that you call them directly on the type.

The usual scenario is to acquire a file handle, open a stream, buffer data to memory and release the handle; with the I/O methods provided most of this is hidden away through encapsulation so that the developer doesn't have to think about it. The downside is that you sometimes don't have the control or flexibility you would need in an application.

The File Class

The methods of the **File** class work well with smaller file sizes; be aware that large files can slow down your application and render your UI unresponsive. The methods in the **File** class are all geared towards reading from files.

You can use the **System.Reflection.Assembly** class to get the assembly working directory.

```
Assembly.GetExecutingAssembly().Location
```

Read From File

The following code sample shows how you can use the **ReadAllText**, **ReadAllLines** and **ReadAllBytes** methods of the **File** class to read from a file.

```
private void ReadFromFile(string path)
{
    string allText = File.ReadAllText(path);
    string[] lineByLine = File.ReadAllLines(path);
    byte[] byteDate = File.ReadAllBytes(path);

    Console.WriteLine("All data");
    Console.WriteLine(allText);

    Console.WriteLine("\nLine by line");
    for (int i = 0; i < lineByLine.Length; i++ )
        Console.WriteLine(String.Format(
            "{0}. {1}", i + 1, lineByLine[i]));

    Console.WriteLine("\nByte data");
    int position = 1;
    foreach (byte b in byteDate)
    {
        Console.Write(String.Format("{0, -4}" ,b));
        if (position == 8)
        {
            Console.WriteLine();
            position = 1;
        }
        else
            position++;
    }
}
```

Write to File

When writing to files, there are two sets of functions you can use; the **Append***xxx* methods add data to the end of an already existing file or create a new file if it does not exist, The **Write***xxx* methods create a new file if it does not exist or overwrites an existing file with the new data.

The following code sample shows how you can use the **WriteAllText**, **WriteAllLines**, **WriteAllBytes**, **AppendAllText** and **AppendAllLines** methods of the **File** class to write data to a file.

```
private void WriteToFile(string path)
{
    string message1 = "Write 1\nWrite 2\nWrite 3";
    File.WriteAllText(path, message1);

    string[] message2 =
        { "Write Line 1\nWrite Line 2\nWrite Line 3" };
    File.WriteAllLines(path, message2);

    byte[] bytes = {
        239, 187, 191, 87, 114, 105, 116, 101,
        32, 98, 121, 116, 101, 115, 32, 49,
        10, 87, 114, 105, 116, 101, 32, 98,
        121, 116, 101, 115, 32, 50, 10, 87,
        114, 105, 116, 101, 32, 98, 121, 116,
        101, 115, 32, 51, };

    File.WriteAllBytes(path, bytes);

    string append1 = "\nAppend 1\nAppend 2\nAppend 3";
    File.AppendAllText(path, append1);

    string[] append2 = {
        "\nAppend Line 1\nAppend Line 2\nAppend Line 3" };
    File.AppendAllLines(path, append2);
}
```

Manipulate Files

Apart from reading and writing to files you also can manipulate them in other ways with the methods in the **File** and **FileInfo** classes. Some of the things you can do with these classes are copy and delete files, and read the file information.

The main difference between the **File** and the **FileInfo** classes is that the **FileInfo** class is instantiated and holds an in-memory representation of the file and can therefore present more metadata about the file.

When copying files with the **Copy** method of the **File** class and the **CopyTo** method of the **FileInfo** class you can choose to have the file overwritten or to have the run-time throw a **System.IO.IOException** if the file already exists.

This sample code shows how to use some of the methods and properties of the **File** and **FileInfo** classes.

```
private void ManipulateFile(string path1, string path2)
{
    bool overwrite = true;

    #region The File class

    File.Copy(path1, path2, overwrite);
    bool fileExist = File.Exists(path2);
    DateTime settingsCreatedOn =
        File.GetCreationTime(path2);

    #endregion

    #region The FileInfo class

    FileInfo fileInfoOriginal = new FileInfo(path1);
    fileInfoOriginal.CopyTo(path2, overwrite);

    FileInfo fileInfo = new FileInfo(path2);
    long length = fileInfo.Length;
    string extension = fileInfo.Extension;
    string directoryPath = fileInfo.DirectoryName;
    bool exist = fileInfo.Exists;
    fileInfo.Delete();

    FileInfo fileInfoAfterDelete = new FileInfo(path2);
    exist = fileInfoAfterDelete.Exists;

    #endregion
}
```

Manipulate Directory

Many applications interact with the file system during a cleanup process or before deleting or checking if a directory exists before manipulating a file. The static **Directory** class and the instance class **DirectoryInfo** provide method for such purposes.

The main difference between the **Directory** and the **DirectoryInfo** classes is that the **DirectoryInfo** class is instantiated and holds an in-memory representation of the directory and can therefore present more metadata about the directory.

When deleting directories you can specify a second parameter in the Delete method that determines if the delete should be recursive that is deleting all the content in the folder including subfolders. If you pass in **false** for this parameter then a **System.IO.IOException** will be thrown if there is any content in the folder you attempt to delete.

This sample code shows how to use some of the methods and properties of the **Directory** and **DirectoryInfo** classes.

Manipulate Paths

When you build an application where you are not certain of what file and directory privileges you will have as a user then you most probably will use the *temp* folder to create and store information. The **Path** class has static methods that you can use to determine the temp folder path and check if the path has an extension, and what that extension is should it have one. You also have the possibility to create temporary filenames that you can use when storing information.

This sample code shows how to use the **Path** class to gain access to the *temp* folder.

```
private void UseTheTempFolder(string path)
{
   // C:\\Users\\UserName\\AppData\\Local\\Temp\\
   string tempDirectoryPath = Path.GetTempPath();

   // true or false
   bool hasExtension = Path.HasExtension(path);

   // .txt, .exe, .dll, ...
   string pathExt = Path.GetExtension(path);

   // C:\\Users\\UserName\\AppData\\Local\\Temp\\
   // tmpE3F3.tmp
   string tempFilePath = Path.GetTempFileName();
}
```

Additional reading: "MSDN Path Class"

Serializing Data

Serialization can be used to persist or transport object data that later can be deserialized back to object instances. We will look at how we can use Binary, XML, JSON and custom serialization/deserialization. The format needs to be lightweight for transportation over HTTP and SOAP.

One scenario could be that you want to save user settings. You could then have an object containing the settings, as properties, be serialized when changing the settings and de-serialized when starting the application. Another scenario could be that you are taking orders from your front-end GUI and the orders are serialized and placed in a queue for later processing. The back-end order processing process will then de-serialize the order data into objects that it can use to store the data.

Binary serialization is often used when transporting objects between applications on the same platform; it is lightweight, has little overhead and preserves fidelity and state between instances.

XML serialization is often used when transporting objects over the SOAP protocol to and from web services; it has overhead because it is verbose since it is formatted using XML, which makes it more processor intensive. The upside is that it can be used cross-platform and between different applications. Another drawback is that it does not preserve type fidelity and only serializes public members. The **System.Runtime.Serialization.Formatters.Soap** assembly has to be referenced.

SOAP XML output example

```
<SOAP-ENV:Envelope xmlns:xsi= ....
   ...
   <Name id="ref-3">Jonas</Name>
   <Age>43</Age>
   ...
</SOAP-ENV:Envelope>
```

JSON serialization is based on a subset of JavaScript and is often used when using asynchronous calls from JavaScript using AJAX. You are not limited to the same domain and JSON is lightweight, human readable, easy to parse and platform independent. The **System.Runtime.Serialization** assembly has to be referenced and a using statement added to **System.**Runtime**.Serialization.Json**.

JSON output example

```
{
   "Name":"Jonas",
   "Age":43
}
```

Making a Class Serializable

To make a class serializable, you have to add some serialization code; add the **[Serializable]** attribute above the class definition and implement the **ISerializable** interface; this interface contain the definition for the method **GetObjectData** that is used when serializing the data. You also need to add a constructor that takes two parameters **SerializationInfo** and **StreamingContext.** This constructor is used when deserializing data to an object. If you want to omit private fields from the serialization process then you add a **[NonSerialized]** to the fields.

This sample code shows how a class can be made serializable.

```
[Serializable]
public class ObjectToSerialize : ISerializable
{
    [NonSerialized]
    private Guid _internalId;
    public int Age { get; set; }
    public string Name { get; set; }

    public ObjectToSerialize()
    {
        _internalId = Guid.NewGuid();
        Name = String.Empty;
        Age = Int32.MinValue;
    }

    public ObjectToSerialize(SerializationInfo info,
    StreamingContext ctxt)
    {
        _internalId = Guid.NewGuid();

        Name = info.GetValue("Name",
            typeof(string)).ToString();

        Age = (int)info.GetValue("Age", typeof(int));
    }

    public void GetObjectData(SerializationInfo info,
    StreamingContext context)
    {
        info.AddValue("Name", Name);
        info.AddValue("Age", Age);
    }
}
```

Binary Serialization

To serialize an object using binary serialization, you need to create an instance of the **BinaryFormatter** class and store it in an **IFormatter** interface pointer. Next, you create the file you want to persist the object to using the **FileStream** class. To serialize the object, you call the **Serialize** method on the **IFormatter** instance passing in the file stream and the object you want to serialize. Do not forget to close the file stream using the **Close** method on the file stream instance.

```
private void SerializeBinary()
{
    ObjectToSerialize obj =
        new ObjectToSerialize("Jonas", 43);

    IFormatter formatter = new BinaryFormatter();
    FileStream file = File.Create(tempDirectoryPath +
        @"\binary.txt");

    formatter.Serialize(file, obj);
    file.Close();
}
```

Binary Deserialization

To deserialize a persisted object to an object instance stored in binary format you need to create an instance of the **BinaryFormatter** class and store it in an **IFormatter** interface pointer. Next you open the file containing the object data you use the **OpenRead** method on the **FileStream** class. To recreate the object you call the **Deserialize** method on the **IFormatter** instance passing in the file stream and storing the result in an instance variable of the serialized type. Do not forget to close the file stream using the **Close** method on the file stream instance.

```
private void DeserializeBinary()
{
    IFormatter formatter = new BinaryFormatter();
    FileStream file = File.OpenRead(tempDirectoryPath +
        @"\binary.txt");

    ObjectToSerialize obj =
        formatter.Deserialize(file) as ObjectToSerialize;

    file.Close();
}
```

XML Serialization

To serialize an object using binary serialization you need to create an instance of the **SoapFormatter** class and store it in an **IFormatter** interface pointer. Next you create the file you want to persist the object to using the **FileStream** class. To serialize the object you call the **Serialize** method on the **IFormatter** instance passing in the file stream and the object you want to serialize. Do not forget to close the file stream using the **Close** method on the file stream instance.

```
private void SerializeXML()
{
    ObjectToSerialize obj =
        new ObjectToSerialize("Jonas", 43);
    IFormatter formatter = new SoapFormatter();
    FileStream file = File.Create(tempDirectoryPath +
        @"\xml.txt");
    formatter.Serialize(file, obj);
    file.Close();
}
```

XML Deserialization

To de-serialize a persisted object to an object instance stored in binary format you need to create an instance of the **SoapFormatter** class and store it in an **IFormatter** interface pointer. Next you open the file containing the object data you use the **OpenRead** method on the **FileStream** class. To recreate the object you call the **Deserialize** method on the **IFormatter** instance passing in the file stream and storing the result in an instance variable of the serialized type. Do not forget to close the file stream using the **Close** method on the file stream instance.

```
private void DeserializeXML()
{
    IFormatter formatter = new SoapFormatter();
    FileStream file = File.OpenRead(tempDirectoryPath +
        @"\xml.txt");
    ObjectToSerialize obj =
        formatter.Deserialize(file) as ObjectToSerialize;
    file.Close(); }
```

JSON Serialization

To serialize an object using binary serialization, you need to create an instance of the DataContractJsonSerializer class and pass in the object type of the class you are serializing. Next you create the file you want to persist the object to using the FileStream class. To serialize the object you call the WriteObject method on the DataContractJsonSerializer instance passing in the file stream and the object you want to serialize. Do not forget to close the file stream using the Close method on the file stream instance.

```
private void SerializeJSON()
{
    ObjectToSerialize obj =
        new ObjectToSerialize("Jonas", 43);

    DataContractJsonSerializer jsonSerializer =
        new DataContractJsonSerializer(obj.GetType());

    FileStream file = File.Create(tempDirectoryPath +
        @"\JSON.txt");

    jsonSerializer.WriteObject(file, obj);
    file.Close();
}
```

JSON Deserialization

To de-serialize a persisted object to an object instance stored in binary format you need to create an instance of the **DataContractJsonSerializer** class passing in the type of the serialized object. Next, you open the file containing the object data you use the **OpenRead** method on the **FileStream** class. To recreate the object, you call the **ReadObject** method on the **DataContractJsonSerializer** instance passing in the file stream and storing the result in an instance variable of the serialized type. Do not forget to close the file stream using the **Close** method on the file stream instance.

```
private void DeserializeJSON()
{
    DataContractJsonSerializer jsonSerializer =
        New DataContractJsonSerializer(
            typeof(ObjectToSerialize));

    FileStream file = File.OpenRead(tempDirectoryPath +
        @"\JSON.txt");

    ObjectToSerialize obj =
        jsonSerializer.ReadObject(file) as
            ObjectToSerialize;
    file.Close();
}
```

The **DataContractJsonSerializer** class inherits from the abstract **XmlObjectSerializer** class and do not implement the **IFormatter** interface.

Custom Serialization

To create a custom serializer, you must implement the **IFormatter** interface located in the **System.**Runtime**.Serialization** namespace. You have to implement the **SurrogateSelector**, **Binder**, and **Context** properties, you do not have to add any code to them just make sure they have a getter and a setter. You must however write code for the **Serialize** and **de-serialize** methods.

The following code samples will show how to implement a custom serializer that saves the object data using the .ini format. In this example, we want the object to serialize and de-serialize itself using the serialize method and the constructor to de-serialize.

The test class

This class is used to test the serialization and de-serialization. First, we use a file stream to create a file that we will use to persist the object. Then we create an instance of the object to persist and call the Serialize method on it passing the file stream as a parameter.

To de-serialize the persisted object, we open the file using a file stream that we pass to the constructor when creating a new instance of the same type that was persisted and store it in an instance variable.

```
public class TestIniFormatter
{
    public TestIniFormatter()
    {
        string tempDirectoryPath = Path.GetTempPath();

        // Serialize
        FileStream serializedFile = File.Create(
            tempDirectoryPath + @"\config.txt");
        IniObject sio = new IniObject("Jonas", 43);
        sio.Serialize(serializedFile);

        // Deserialize
        FileStream deserializedFile = File.OpenRead(
            tempDirectoryPath + @"\config.txt");
        IniObject dio = new IniObject(deserializedFile);
    }
}
```

The IniObject Class

This is the class that we will persist instances of; it contains a public **Serialize** method and a private **Deserialize** method that is called from the constructor that takes a file stream as a parameter. The class is decorated with the **[Serializable]** attribute to make it serializable.

The **Serialize** method use an instance of the custom formatter and calls the **Serialize** method on the instance passing in the file stream and the current object instance with the **this** keyword.

The **Deserialize** method uses an instance of the custom formatter and calls the **Deserialize** method on the instance passing in the file stream casting it to the current object type. Then it sets the properties with the de-serialized values.

```
[Serializable]
public class IniObject
{
    public int Age { get; set; }
    public string Name { get; set; }

    public IniObject()
    {
        Name = String.Empty;
        Age = Int32.MinValue;
    }
    public IniObject(string name, int age)
    {
        Name = name;
        Age = age;
    }
    public IniObject(FileStream file)
    {
        Name = String.Empty;
        Age = Int32.MinValue;
        Deserialize(file);
    }
    public void Serialize(FileStream file)
    {
        SerializationUsingCustomFormatter ini =
            new SerializationUsingCustomFormatter();
        ini.Serialize(file, this);
        file.Close();
    }
    private void Deserialize(FileStream file)
    {
        SerializationUsingCustomFormatter ini =
            new SerializationUsingCustomFormatter();
        IniObject data =
            (IniObject)ini.Deserialize(file);
        file.Close();
        this.Name = data.Name;
        this.Age = data.Age;
    }
}
```

The Custom Formatter

This is the custom formatter class that implements the **IFormatter** interface; it will be used to serialize and de-serialize objects. The constructor creates an instance of the **StreamingContext** class that determines the context for streaming data when serializing and de-serializing.

The helper method **GetType** will return the type of the persisted object from the passed-in stream reader. The type is stored on the first row of the file as a property named "@ClassName". The type value is parsed from the first line.

In the **Serialize** method, we use the **FormatterServices.GetSerializableMembers** method to fetch the members that will be serialized from the passed-in object in the graph parameter. Then we use the **FormatterServices.GetObjectData** method to fetch the member values. Lastly, we write the object type on the first row of the file and loop in the rest of the member names and values; the values are stored as key-value pair.

In the **Deserialize** method, we open the file containing the persisted data using a stream reader. Then we call the GetType helper method to get the correct type to store the data in; we pass in the type to the **FormatterServices.GetUninitializedObject** method to create a new instance of the persisted type. Then we call the **FormatterServices.GetSerializableMembers** method passing in the instance we created to fetch its serializable members. The Dictionary instance is used to store the members and their values as key-value pairs when we loop over the persisted data. When we have all the members and their values, we loop over the dictionary and convert the member names and types into real data types using the **Convert.ChangeType** method. The last thing we do is to populate the object with the member data using the **FormatterServices.PopulateObjectMembers** method and return it.

Custom formatter output example

```
@ClassName=Samples.IniObject

<Age>k__BackingField=43

<Name>k__BackingField=Jonas
```

```
public class SerializationUsingCustomFormatter :
IFormatter
{
    private readonly char _delimiter = '=' ;
    public ISurrogateSelector SurrogateSelector
    { get; set; }
    public SerializationBinder Binder { get; set; }
    public StreamingContext Context { get; set; }

    public SerializationUsingCustomFormatter()
    {
        this.Context = new StreamingContext(
            StreamingContextStates.All);
    }

    public object Deserialize(
    Stream serializationStream)
    {
        StreamReader buffer =
            new StreamReader(serializationStream);

        Type typeToDeserialize = this.GetType(buffer);

        Object obj = FormatterServices
        .GetUninitializedObject(typeToDeserialize);

        MemberInfo[] members =
            FormatterServices.GetSerializableMembers(
                obj.GetType(), this.Context);

        Dictionary<string, object> serializedMemberData =
            new Dictionary<string, object>();
```

```
    while (buffer.Peek() >= 0)
    {
        string line = buffer.ReadLine();
        string[] sarr = line.Split(_delimiter);
        serializedMemberData.Add(
        sarr[0].Trim(), // Variable name.
        sarr[1].Trim()); // Variable value.
    }

    buffer.Close();

    List<object> dataAsCorrectTypes =
        new List<object>();

    for (int i = 0; i < members.Length; i++)
    {
        FieldInfo field = members[i] as FieldInfo;

        if (!serializedMemberData.ContainsKey(
            field.Name)) throw new
                SerializationException(field.Name);

        // Change the type of the value to the
        // member type
        object valueAsCorrectType =
            Convert.ChangeType(
                serializedMemberData[field.Name],
                field.FieldType);

        dataAsCorrectTypes.Add(valueAsCorrectType);
    }

    // Populate the object with the deserialized
    // values.
    return FormatterServices.PopulateObjectMembers(
        obj, members, dataAsCorrectTypes.ToArray());
}
```

```
    public void Serialize(Stream serializationStream,
    object graph)
    {
        MemberInfo[] allMembers =
            FormatterServices.GetSerializableMembers(
                graph.GetType(), this.Context);

            object[] fieldData =
                FormatterServices.GetObjectData(
                    graph, allMembers);

            StreamWriter sw =
                new StreamWriter(serializationStream);

            sw.WriteLine("@ClassName{0}{1}", _delimiter,
                graph.GetType().FullName);

            for (int i = 0; i < fieldData.Length; ++i)
            {
                sw.WriteLine("{0}{1}{2}",
                    // Member name.
                    allMembers[i].Name,
                    _delimiter,
                    // Member value.
                    fieldData[i].ToString());
            }

            sw.Close();
    }

    private Type GetType(StreamReader buffer)
    {
        string nameOfClass = buffer.ReadLine().Split(
            new char[] { _delimiter })[1];

        return Type.GetType(nameOfClass);
    }
}
```

Using Streams

When a file, whether in a file system or on a web server fetched over HTTP, reaches a certain size you no longer can use an atomic operation to manipulate the whole file in memory; this is where file streams come into the picture. By streaming a file, you can manipulate it in chunks. A file stream is a sequence of bytes.

Streams are typically used to read data onto a byte array or other types, or fetch data from types and write it to a stream. You can query the stream for the current position when performing reads or writes.

When choosing the stream type, you need to consider what type of data you are manipulating (binary, text ...) and where it is or will be stored; on a web server, in memory or in a file system. The most common file streams are stored in the **System.IO** namespace.

All stream classes derive from the **Stream** class; it contains the most commonly used functionality. An instance of the **Stream** class holds a pointer that refers to the current position in the data source; when first created, the pointer points to the byte before the fist byte in the data source. The pointer is then advanced when reading from or writing to the stream.

When using streams, you cannot use the **Stream** class directly, instead you use one of the specialized stream classes such as **FileStream** to connect to a file in a file system, **MemoryStream** storing data in memory, or a **NetworkStream** to connect to a data source on a network source.

The **StreamReader/StreamWriter** reads/writes textual data. The **BinaryReader/BinaryWriter** reads/writes binary data. All these readers and writers use streams like the **FileStream**, **MemoryStream** and the

NetworkStream to connect to a source.

Streams and binary data

Reading binary data is fast and takes up less space when stored; the drawback is that it is not readable.

Reading binary data

The **BinaryReader** class has several properties and functions that you can use when reading from a stream. The **Read** method reads the remaining bytes in the stream from a specific position. The **ReadByte** and **ReadBytes** methods read the next byte or a number of bytes. The **Close** method closes the **BinaryReader** instance and its underlying stream. The **BaseStream** property makes it possible to access the underlying stream.

This code sample shows three ways you can read from a file using a **BinaryReader**.

```
private void BinaryReaderTest()
{
    FileStream sourceFile = new FileStream(binaryPath,
        FileMode.Open, FileAccess.Read);
    BinaryReader reader = new BinaryReader(sourceFile);
    int length = (int)reader.BaseStream.Length;

    // Read all data into an array
    byte[] binaryData = new byte[length];
    reader.Read(binaryData, 0, length);

    // Read data with a while loop
    sourceFile.Position = 0;
    byte[] binaryData1 = new byte[length];
    while (sourceFile.Position < length)
        binaryData1[sourceFile.Position] =
            reader.ReadByte();
```

```
// Read data with a for loop
    sourceFile.Position = 0;
    byte[] binaryData2 = new byte[length];
    for (int i = 0; i < length; i++)
        binaryData2[i] = reader.ReadByte();

    reader.Close();
    sourceFile.Close();
}
```

Writing binary data

The **BinaryWriter** class has several properties and functions that you can use when writing to a stream. The **Write** method writes to the stream and advances the pointer. The **Seek** method makes it possible to position the pointer at a specific position; you can then write to that byte. The **Flush** method makes it possible to write the remaining bytes in the buffer to the stream. The **Close** method closes the **BinaryWriter** instance and its underlying stream. The **BaseStream** property makes it possible to access the underlying stream.

This code sample shows how you can write to a file using a **Binary-Writer**.

```
private void BinaryWriterTest()
{
    byte[] binaryData = { 1, 2, 4, 8, 16, 32, 64, 128 };

    FileStream destinationFile =
        new FileStream(binaryPath, FileMode.Create,
            FileAccess.Write);

    BinaryWriter writer =
        new BinaryWriter(destinationFile);

    foreach (byte data in binaryData)
        writer.Write(data);

    writer.Close();
    destinationFile.Close();
}
```

Streams and text data

When you need to store and read human readable data, you can use the **StreamReader** and **StreamWriter** classes.

Reading text data

The **StreamReader** class has several properties and functions that you can use when reading from a stream. The **Peak** method reads the next character, but does not consume it. The **Read** method reads the next character as a binary delivered as an int; you might have to explicitly convert the value. The **ReadBlock** method makes it possible to read a block of characters from a specified position. The **ReadLine** method makes it possible to read a line of characters from the stream. The **ReadToEnd** method makes it possible to read the remaining characters from the current position. The **Close** method closes the **StreamReader** instance and its underlying stream. The **EndOfStream** property tells you if you have reached the end of the stream.

This code sample shows how you can read from a file using a **Stream-Reader**.

```
private void StreamReaderTest()
{
    FileStream sourceFile = new FileStream(textPath,
        FileMode.Open, FileAccess.Read);

    StreamReader reader = new StreamReader(sourceFile);

    StringBuilder text = new StringBuilder();

    while (reader.Peek() != -1)
        text.Append((char)reader.Read());

    string data = text.ToString();

    reader.Close();
    sourceFile.Close();
}
```

Writing text data

The **StreamWriter** class has several properties and functions that you can use when reading from a stream. The **Flush** method writes the remaining data in the buffer to the stream. The **Write** method writes the data to the stream and advances the stream. The **WriteLine** method writes the data to the stream followed by a new line break. The **Close** method closes the **StreamWriter** instance and its underlying stream.

The **AutoFlush** property tells the **StreamWriter** to flush data to the stream after every time it writes data. With the **NewLine** property you can decide which characters that will be used to represent a new line break.

This code sample shows how you can write to a file using a **Stream-Writer**.

```
private void StreamWriterTest()
{
    string data = "This text is human readable.";

    FileStream destinationFile = new FileStream(
        textPath, FileMode.Create, FileAccess.Write);

    StreamWriter writer =
        new StreamWriter(destinationFile);

    writer.WriteLine(data);

    writer.Close();
    destinationFile.Close();
}
```

Database Access

16

In Visual Studio 2012 and .NET Framework, we can use *Entity Data Models (EDM)* to access data in a database; we can then use *Language-Integrated Query (LINQ)* to query the database.

ADO.NET Entity Framework removes worries that you might have had in the past about type- and syntax checking at compile time, and returns containing untyped data records by introducing EDMs. The data access code is type- and syntax-checked at compile-time.

You can use inheritance and relationship enabled conceptual models instead of the traditional normalized model when writing applications that access data using the ADO.NET Entity Framework. You no longer have to have a deep understanding of the database structure in order to write applications that access data. You do not have to rewrite or redistribute all your data access code if you want to target a different storage model and you can write code that is not dependent on a specific data storage system.

Database tables and queries are mapped to .NET Framework objects using EDMs. To manipulate and query EDMs constructs, you use *Entity Structured Query Language (Entity SQL)*. Within a conceptual model, you can work with *Common Language Runtime (CLR)* objects through the *Object Services*.

The conceptual model describes the semantics from a business standpoint; it defines entities and relationships with a business sense. The model is then mapped to the data source through the logic data model of the underlying data.

Additional reading: "ADO.NET Entity Framework"

ADO.NET Entity Data Model Tools

When creating EDMs using the ADO.NET Entity Data Model Tools, you can use either of the *database-first* or the *code-first* designs. With the *database-first* design, you create the database first or use an existing database before generating your model; this design can limit the flexibility in the long run. With the *code-first* design, you create the entities for your application before creating the database; this design is often preferred by developers because the business functionality is part of the application design.

Wizards

Apart from the *Entity Data Model Designer* that you can use to graphically create and relate entities in a model, there are three wizards you can use when working with models.

The *Entity Data Model Wizard* uses a *database-first* design method to create a new conceptual model from an existing source.

The *Update Model Wizard* can be used to update an existing conceptual model with changes from the underlying data source.

The *Generate Database Wizard* uses a *code-first* design method to create a new database from a conceptual design built with the *Entity Data Model Designer*.

Additional reading: "ADO.NET Entity Data Model Tools"

Create an EDM from an Existing Database

1. In the Solution Explorer right-click on the project where you want the model to be added.

2. Select **Add-New Item** in the context menu that is displayed.

3. In the *Add New Item* dialog box click the **Data** tab in the **Visual C#** section.

4. Select **ADO.NET Entity Data Model** in the list.

5. Give the model a name in the **Name** field.

6. Click the **Add** button.

7. Select the **Generate from database** option.

8. Click the **Next** button.

9. If you find the correct connection in the drop-down list then select it, otherwise click the **New Connection** button.

    a. If you use Microsoft SQL Server then make sure that the Data source field contains the text: *Microsoft SQL Server (SqlClient);* otherwise click the **Change** button and select the appropriate option.

    b. Enter *(localdb)\v11.0* in the **Server name** field.

    c. Select a database in the **Select or enter a database name** drop-down list.

    d. Click the **Test Connection** button to make sure that the connection works.

    e. Click the **OK** button to close the *Connection Properties* dialog box.

10. Click the **Next** button.

11. Select the database objects that you want to include in the model.

12. Click the **Finish** button.

If you want to see the generated C# code for the model then:

1. Expand the *modelname*.edmx in the Solution Explorer.
2. Under the *modelname*.edmx expand *modelname.context.tt*.
3. Click on the *modelname.context.cs*.
4. Expand *modelname.tt* to find the entity C# files.

Extending a Generated Entity Class

You can add business logic to the model classes; it is recommended that you write the logic in another class with the same name as the model class declared with the **partial** keyword. The model classes are declared as **partial** for this scenario so that you can extend them. It is imperative that you place the extension in a .cs file separate from the entity class it extends, otherwise it will be overwritten when the model is regenerated.

In this code sample, we extend the Student class with a method that calculates the age of the student.

The generated **Student** class.

```
public partial class Student
{
   public int Id { get; set; }
   public string FirstName { get; set; }
   public string LastName { get; set; }
   public System.DateTime DateOfBirth { get; set; }
   ...
}
```

The extended **Student** class located in another .cs file.

```
public partial class Student
{
    public int GetAge()
    {
        DateTime DOB = (DateTime)DateOfBirth;
        TimeSpan difference = DateTime.Now.Subtract(DOB);
        int ageInYears = (int)(difference.Days / 365.25);
        return ageInYears;
    }
}
```

Additional reading: "Partial Classes and Methods (C# Programming Guide)"

Reading and Modifying Data

Among the generated classes you will find a class that makes it possible to query and work with entity data objects located in the *modelname*.**Context.cs** file; the class inherits from the **System.Data.Entity.DbContext** class and uses the connection string provided by the wizard in the **App.Config** file to modify or fetch data.

Each entity in the model will be represented by a **DbSet<TEntity>** class; this class can be used to read, create, update and delete data.

The following code shows the entities class in the *modelname*.**Context.cs** file for the School example.

```
public partial class SchoolDBEntities : DbContext
{
    public SchoolDBEntities() :
        base("name=SchoolDBEntities") { }

    public DbSet<Student> Student { get; set; }
    public DbSet<Teacher> Teacher { get; set; }
}
```

To manipulate data you need to create an instance of the class inheriting from the DbContext class; from that instance you then have access to the entities, for instance Student, that map to the data source. You can then loop over the **DbSet** and fetch each Student.

In this sample code, we read data using the database context and call the **GetAge** method that we extended the **Student** entity with.

```
private void GetStudents()
{
    SchoolDBEntities DBContext = new SchoolDBEntities();
    foreach (School.Student student in DBContext.Student)
    {
        Console.WriteLine("{0} {1} {2}",
            student.FirstName, student.LastName,
            student.GetAge());
    }
}
```

In this sample code, we change the last name of one of the students using the database context. Remember to call the **SaveChanges** method to persist the changes to the data source.

```
private void AlterStudent(string lastName,
string newLastName)
{
    SchoolDBEntities DBContext = new SchoolDBEntities();
    var student = DBContext.Student.First(
        e => e.LastName == lastName);
    if (student != null)
    {
        student.LastName = newLastName;
    }
    DBContext.SaveChanges();
}
```

Additional reading: “DbSet<TEntity> Class” and “MSDN Enumerable Methods”

Querying Data Using LINQ

LINQ is a query language that can be used to query a number of data sources. LINQ is built into .NET Languages such as Visual C# and has standardized, declarative query syntax. You can use LINQ to query data sources such as Collections, ADO.NET dataset, SQL Server databases and XML documents; that is any data source that implements the **IEnumerable** interface.

In this chapter, we will explore how to query data in an *Entity Data Model (EDM)* using LINQ.

You use the following basic syntax when querying with LINQ:

```
from <variable names> in <data source>
group <grouping criteria>
where <selection criteria>
orderby <result ordering criteria>
select <variable name>
```

If you want to iterate over the result you can store it in a variable of type **IQueryable<T>**. The following code sample shows how you can iterate over **IQueryable<T>**.

```
private void PrintStudents(IQueryable<Student> students)
{
    foreach (Student student in students)
        Console.WriteLine("{0,-10}{1,-10}{2,-3}",
            student.FirstName, student.LastName,
            student.GetAge());
}
```

Selecting Data

When selecting data, the minimum syntax that you need is from ... in ... select this will give you the all the data from the data source. Often when selecting data you do not want to execute the LINQ statement at once but rather manipulate it further before executing it. To do this, you store the fetched data in a variable of type **IQueryable<T>**. If you want to force the execution of the LINQ statement, you can call one of the following methods **ToList**, **ToArray**, or **ToDictionary**.

The following ample code shows how you can select data from an EDM using a LINQ statement.

```
private void Select()
{
    SchoolDBEntities DBContext = new SchoolDBEntities();
    IQueryable<Student> student =
        from s in DBContext.Student
        select s;

    PrintStudents(student);
}
```

Where

If you want to filter the result and select a subset of the data in the data source, you use a **where** clause; for instance selecting all the students who are younger than 10 years old. Note that we can't use the **DateTime** type with LINQ when querying EDMs; instead we use the **EntityFunctions** class.

```
private void Where()
{
    SchoolDBEntities DBContext = new SchoolDBEntities();

IQueryable<Student> student =
        from s in DBContext.Student
        where (int)(EntityFunctions.DiffDays(
            s.DateOfBirth, DateTime.Now) / 365.25) < 10
        select s;
```

```
    PrintStudents(student);
}
```

Orderby

If you want to sort the result in ascending or descending order based on one or more of the returned fields, you use the **orderby** keyword.

```
private void OrderBy()
{
    IQueryable<Student> student =
        from s in DBContext.Student
        orderby s.LastName ascending
        select s;

    PrintStudents(student);
}
```

Store Data in a New Class

If you want to store a subset of the values in each of the returned items when querying with LINQ, you can create a class that will be the model for the new objects that will be created. You use the **new** keyword followed by the class name when doing the **select**.

In the following code sample, we use a subset of the student data to create new objects containing the data using the **StudentPart** class. When the query is executed, the result will contain objects of the **StudentPart** class.

```
class StudentPart
{
    public string FullName { get; set; }
    public DateTime DOB { get; set; }
}
```

```
class LINQandEDM
{
    private void NewClass()
    {
        SchoolDBEntities DBContext =
            new SchoolDBEntities();

        IQueryable<StudentPart> student =
            from s in DBContext.Student
            select new StudentPart
            {
                FullName = s.FirstName + " " +
                    s.LastName,
                DOB = s.DateOfBirth
            };
    }
}
```

Group – Aggregating Data

You can aggregate data using a **Group** clause in the LINQ statement. To aggregate means to group data that belong to the same category and perform a task on the grouped data; this could, for instance, be to calculate the number of items that fit the criteria.

The following code sample shows how we can find out how many students there are in each class. We store the aggregated data in an anonymous object; an object that has no predefined data type.

```
private void AggregatingData()
{
    var studentsInClass =
        from student in DBContext.Student
        group student by student.ClassId into sGroup
        select new
        {
            Class = sGroup.Key,
            NumberOfStudents = sGroup.Count()
        };
}
```

Navigate Related Entities

If two entities have a relation defined between them you can navigate to the related entity and use its data from the first entity. Let's say that we wanted to find out the name of a student's teacher, we could then easily access the Teacher entity, related to the Student entity, from the Student entity.

The following code sample shows how we can combine data from the Student and Teacher entity using the fact that they have a relation and store the result in an anonymous object. We are interested only in the first student, so we use the **First** method to fetch only the first item in the data source.

```
private void NavigateRelatedEntities()
{
    var studentInfo = (
        from student in DBContext.Student
        select new
        {
            Teacher = student.Teacher.FirstName + " " +
                student.Teacher.LastName,
                Class = student.Teacher.Class,
                Student = student.FirstName + " " +
                student.LastName,
        }).First();

    Console.WriteLine(
        "Student: {0}, Class: {1}, Teacher: {2}",
        studentInfo.Student, studentInfo.Class,
        studentInfo.Teacher);
}
```

Forcing Execution

If you want to execute a LINQ statement immediately, you cannot store it in an **IQueryable<T>**, instead you have to store it in an appropriate data type. You can force execution by calling one of the following methods **ToList**, **ToArray**, or **ToDictionary**.

The following code sample shows how we can force execution storing the result immediately in an **IList** instance variable by calling the **ToList** method. Note that you have to enclose the LINQ statement in parenthesis and call the method on the whole expression within the parenthesis.

```
private void ForcingExecution()
{
    IList<Student> student = (
        from s in DBContext.Student
        select s).ToList();
}
```

Web Services

Access to data over the web can be achieved by using web services or other application programming interfaces (APIs). You need methods to connect to these services and APIs and receive messages and send data. We will look at how it can be done with a data-driven web service that exposes data through an Entity Data Model (EDM), and how a file can be uploaded to an FTP site using the *File Transfer Protocol (FTP)*.

We will start by looking at how we can send and receive data without a reference set to the web service, and then how we can use a *Representational State Transfer (REST)* service to do the same.

When communicating with remote data sources, be it a web service, an FTP or a different method, the .NET Framework uses *requests* and *responses* to handle the messages. This is done by first establishing a connection to the remote source and sending a request, which can contain any required data, to the remote data source. Then the application has to wait for the response. Note that you, as a developer, do not have any control over how long it takes. When the response is available, you can process the returned data.

There are several request and response classes in the System.Net namespace that target different data sources such as http, ftp and files.

The **WebRequest** class is an abstract class that all the other request classes derive from; it contains the base functionality to request information using a Uniform Resource Identifier (URI). The **WebResponse** class is an abstract class from which all the other response classes derive; it contains the base functionality to process any response from a URI.

HttpWebRequest	Contains functionality to handle an HTTP web request.
HttpWebResponse	Contains functionality to process an HTTP web response.
FtpWebRequest	Contains functionality to handle an FTP web request.
FtpWebResponse	Contains functionality to process an FTP web response.
FileWebRequest	Contains functionality to request files.
FileWebResponse	Contains functionality to process a file web response.

You do **not** have to use both a request and response message, using only a request is known as a one-way operation.

Additional reading: "System.Net Namespace"

WCF Service

When you do not want a data-driven, highly coupled web service that uses the entities from the data source EDM as types, then a WCF Service is a good choice. In a **WCF Service,** you define the *service contract* by creating an interface that will be used when implementing the service class in the .svc file; the methods defined in the interface must be decorated with the **OperationContract** if you want to use it from a client. The classes you define needs to be decorated with the **DataContract** attribute.

It is fully possible to use a data source and an EDM in a WCF Service; however, it is going to be loosely coupled, meaning that you need to use the EDM in a more direct way in your methods.

Create a WCF Service

Before we have a look at sending a receiving data from a WCF Service, we will examine how we can create a new WCF Service.

1. In Visual Studio 2012, select **File-New Project** or click the **New Project** link on the start page.
2. In the *New Project* dialog, click the **Web** tab to the left and select **ASP.NET Empty Web Application**.
3. Give the service a name in the **Name** text box and click **OK**.
4. Right click on the WCF Service project and select **Add-New Item**.
5. In the *Add New Item* dialog, you click on the **Web** tab and select **WCF Service**.
6. Give the service a name in the **Name** text box and click **OK**.

Service Contract

The **service contract** determines what will be implemented in your WCF Service and what can be used from the client. You implement the service contract as an interface that is implemented in the web service class that is exposed to the client.

Each member that you want to expose to the client must be decorated with the **OperationContract** attribute.

The following code sample shows how to implement a service contract that exposed a method that returns a list of student that has a specific last name.

```
[ServiceContract]
public interface ISchoolService
{
    [OperationContract]
    IList<WCFStudent> StudentByLastName(string lastName);
}
```

Data Contract

If you create a web service that uses a custom object, you need to define the class and its members accordingly with the appropriate attribute decorations. The class must be decorated with the **Data-Contract** attribute and the members with the **DataMember** attribute; the attributes are located in the *System.Runtime.Serialization* name-space. Using these attributes exposes the object and its members from the web service; this makes it possible for the serialization process to transport the data in formats such as *XML* or *JavaScript Object Notation (JSON)*.

The following code sample shows how to use the attributes.

```
[DataContract]
public class WCFStudent
{
    [DataMember]
    public int id { get; set; }
    [DataMember]
    public string FristName { get; set; }
    [DataMember]
    public string LastName { get; set; }
    [DataMember]
    public DateTime DateOfBirth { get; set; }
    [DataMember]
    public string Class { get; set; }
    [DataMember]
    public string Teacher { get; set; }
}
```

Additional reading: "DataContractAttribute Class"

The Service Class

After adding the desired data source by creating an EDM for it, you implement the method that will fetch the students matching the passed-in last name. When you create the EDM, you will be prompted to give a name for the *Entity connection settings (SchoolDBEntities)*. This will be the name of the class that you use to establish a connection, or a context, to the EDM; you use an instance of this class in the method to fetch the desired data.

The following code sample shows how to implement the method that the client calls in the web service class; note that the class implements the **service contract** interface. Note also that we use data from both the **Student** and the **Teacher** entity when populating the **WCFStudent** instance.

```
public class SchoolService : ISchoolService
{
    public IList<WCFStudent> StudentByLastName(
    string lastName)
    {
        SchoolDBEntities entities =
            new SchoolDBEntities();

        return (from s in entities.Student
                where s.LastName == lastName
                select new WCFStudent
                {
                    id = s.Id,
                    FristName = s.FirstName,
                    LastName = s.LastName,
                    DateOfBirth = s.DateOfBirth,
                    Class = s.Teacher.Class,
                    Teacher = s.Teacher.FirstName + " " +
                        s.Teacher.LastName
                }).ToList();
    }
}
```

The Client Call to the WCF Service

In the client, you need to set a reference to the WCF Service; you do this by right clicking on the **References** folder and selecting **Add Service Reference**. Make sure to give it a name that corresponds to the functionality that the service provides.

Once the reference has been added, we can call the WCF Service to fetch the student data; we do this by using the namespace name followed by the service name to create an instance of the service proxy, the context. On this context object, we then call the method.

After you have changed anything in a WCF Service that is referenced from the client, you can right click on the WCF Service project and select **clear** before building the service again; this will remove any temporary files that can potentially cause problems when referencing the service from a client.

On the client, you can remove the reference to the service, right click the project and select clear before adding the reference to the service again; this to make sure that old debug information is not causing problems when adding the reference.

The following code sample shows one way to implement the service call from the client.

```
public void CallService()
{
    WCFEDMServiceReference.SchoolServiceClient context =
        new WCFEDMServiceReference.SchoolServiceClient();

    IList<WCFEDMServiceReference.WCFStudent> students =
        context.StudentByLastName("Smith");
}
```

WCF Service Returning JSON (Request/Response)

What we want to achieve is to send object data in JSON format from the WCF Service to the client and convert the JSON back into objects on the client.

You can read how to create a WCF Service in the Create a WCF Service section. The sample uses the name *WCFJsonService* for the WCF Service;

this will create the *IWCFSchoolService* interface that is implemented by the *WCFJsonSchoolService* web service class.

We want to use a data source to return data from a Microsoft SQL Server database; you can read how to add an Entity Data Model to a project in the Create an EDM from an Existing Database section. The sample uses the name *SchoolModel* for the EDM and *SchoolDBEntities* for the entity connection; the latter class is used to create the data source context that connects to the data source.

To send *JSON* data instead of the *Atom Feed* that is the default data transfer method, you need to make a few changes to the *Web.Config* file and add a couple of assembly references.

The references that you need to add are **System.run-time.Serialization** to handle JSON data and **System.ServiceModel.Web** to handle the web method attributes that we need.

Web.Config JSON Settings

The additions have to be made to the *Web.Config* file.

```
<system.serviceModel>
    <services>
        <service
            behaviorConfiguration="RestServiceBehavior"
            name="WCFJsonService.WCFSchoolService">
                <endpoint address=""
                    behaviorConfiguration="web"
                    binding="webHttpBinding"
                    bindingConfiguration=
                        "webHttpBindingWithJSONP"
                    contract=
                    "WCFJsonService.IWCFSchoolService"
                />
        </service>
    </services>
```

```
    <bindings>
        <webHttpBinding>
            <binding name="webHttpBindingWithJSONP" />
        </webHttpBinding>
    </bindings>

    <behaviors>
        <endpointBehaviors>
            <behavior name="web">
                <webHttp />
            </behavior>
        </endpointBehaviors>

        <serviceBehaviors>
            <behavior name="RestServiceBehavior">
                <serviceMetadata httpGetEnabled="true" />
                <serviceDebug
                includeExceptionDetailInFaults="false"/>
            </behavior>
            <behavior name="">
                <serviceMetadata httpGetEnabled="true"
                    httpsGetEnabled="true" />
                <serviceDebug
                includeExceptionDetailInFaults="false" />
            </behavior>
        </serviceBehaviors>
    </behaviors>

    <serviceHostingEnvironment
        aspNetCompatibilityEnabled="true"
        multipleSiteBindingsEnabled="true" />

</system.serviceModel>
```

The Service Interface

The methods that we want to be able to use from the client must be defined in the *IWCFSchoolService* interface. Each method must be decorated with the **OperationsContract** attribute and for a method to be able to fetch data, it must be decorated with the **WebGet** attribute; in the **WebGet** attribute we can specify any parameters that needs to be passed to the method as well as the format the data will be serialized with.

We will also create a **DataContract** class that will act as a model for the serialized data; you could off course place this class in a separate .cs file if you like. The important things to keep in mind are that the class must be decorated with the DataContract attribute and the members of the class must be decorated with the DataMember attribute. You can see the data contract class in the Data Contract section.

```
[ServiceContract]
public interface IWCFJsonSchoolService
{
    [WebGet(UriTemplate =
        "StudentsByLastName?lastName={lastName}",
        ResponseFormat = WebMessageFormat.Json)]
    [OperationContract]
    IList<WCFStudent> StudentsByLastName(string lastName);
}
```

The Service Class

The method that we defined in the interface needs to be implemented in *WCFSchoolService* class; this class is called from the client when performing a web request.

The *StudentsByLastName* method in this sample code show how you can connect to the data source and fetch data that are streamed as JSON back to the client.

```
public class WCFJsonSchoolService : IWCFJsonSchoolService
{
    public IList<WCFStudent> StudentsByLastName(
    string lastName)
    {
        SchoolDBEntities entities =
            new SchoolDBEntities();
```

```
        return (
            from s in entities.Student
            where s.LastName == lastName
            select new WCFStudent
            {
                id = s.Id,
                FristName = s.FirstName,
                LastName = s.LastName,
                DateOfBirth = s.DateOfBirth,
                Class = s.Teacher.Class,
                Teacher = s.Teacher.FirstName + " " +
                    s.Teacher.LastName
            }).ToList<WCFStudent>();
    }
}
```

The Client

From the client we want to call the WCF Service and parse the returned stream back into objects; this could be done in a number of ways, but we will use the **DataContractJsonSerializer** class located in the **System.run-time.Serialization** assembly. To spice things up a bit, we will create a **Converter** class in which we will create an extension method that converts the JSON stream to objects.

To call the web service, we use an **HttpWebRequest** and to get the stream from the **HttpWebResponse** instance we use the **GetResponse-Stream** method; we then convert that stream using our extension method and save the list in the *students* variable. Create the **ReadFrom-JsonService** method in the main **Program** class and call it from the **Main** method.

```
private static void ReadFromJsonService()
{
    HttpWebRequest service =
        (HttpWebRequest)WebRequest.Create(webServiceUri +
            "StudentsByLastName?lastName=Smith");

    var response = service.GetResponse() as
        HttpWebResponse;
```

```
    var students = response.GetResponseStream()
        .Deserialize<List<Student>>();

    response.Close();
}
```

The URI

Add a static variable that holds the web service URI in the main Program class. Important to note is that the port number must be the same as the web service. You can find the port number in the web service project *Properties* window under the **Web** tab in the **Project URI** field.

```
private static readonly string webServiceUri =
   "http://localhost:3516/WCFJsonSchoolService.svc/";
```

The Model Class

Because we do not have access to the data model in the web service we have to create one in the client project; the easiest way is to look at the returned data and determine the property types.

The object model will be used when de-serializing the JSON objects sent from the web service.

```
public class Student
{
    public int id { get; set; }
    public string FirstName { get; set; }
    public string LastName { get; set; }
    public DateTime DateOfBirth { get; set; }
    public string Class { get; set; }
    public string Teacher { get; set; }
}
```

The Converter Class

Create a new class and name it **Converter**; it must be declared as **public static** because the .NET run-time demands that extension methods be placed in a public static class. If the Converter class is located in a different namespace than the application, you have to add a using statement to its namespace to the application class.

Extension methods are a little bit different that ordinary methods in that they operate on the type instance directly and extend the functionality without changing the actual type. This makes it possible to write extended functionality for types that cannot be inherited or that you do not want to inherit.

An extension method must be declared as **public static** to be reachable anywhere; it always contain at least one parameter and the first parameter must be declared using the **this** keyword and be of the type that you are extending.

In the sample code below we use the **DataContractJsonSerializer** class to convert a stream containing JSON objects into objects of the model class (Student) that we defined earlier.

```
public static class Converter
{
    public static T Deserialize<T>(this Stream json)
    {
        using (MemoryStream ms =
            new MemoryStream(Encoding.Unicode.GetBytes(
            new StreamReader(json).ReadToEnd())))
        {
            DataContractJsonSerializer serializer =
                new DataContractJsonSerializer(typeof(T));
            return (T)serializer.ReadObject(ms);
        }
    }
}
```

WCF Data Service (Request/Response)

In this section we will have a look at how we can use the **HttpWebRequest** and **HttpWebResponse** classes to fetch and update data using a WCF Data Service as well as how we can upload a file to an FTP site using the **FtpWebRequest** and **FtpWebResponse** classes.

The first thing you need to do when using an HTTP request to a web service is to get the URI to the web service and the method you want to call. Next, you use the **WebRequest** class to create an **HttpWebRequest**, note that we are not using the **HttpWebRequest** class to create the request object. Use the **GetResponse** method on the request object to fetch the response and store it in an **HttpWebResponse** object. Use the members of the response object to process the response; you can use the **StatusCode** property to find out if a response that is sent back is OK.

The same steps are used for the other data source protocols, for instance, for FTP just use the FtpWebRequest and FtpWebResponse classes instead.

```
Var uri =
"http://school.SourceCodeAcademy.com/SchoolService.svc/
   GetStudentsByLastName";

var request = WebRequest.Create(uri) as HttpWebRequest;
var response = request.GetResponse() as HttpWebResponse;

// Returns OK if you get a response back.
var status = response.StatusCode;
```

Network Exceptions

When calling a remote service, you cannot be sure that it will be running to process your request; if it is not then you need to be prepared for that in your code. The **GetResponse** method will throw different exceptions depending on what has gone wrong so be sure to catch exceptions of type **WebException** and check the message using a **try/ catch** statement.

If the service is not online, you can expect the message: *WebException – The remote server returned an error: (404) Not Found.*

If you do not have the right credentials when you try to access a service, you can expect the message: *WebException – The remote server returned an error: 401 unauthorized.*

Authentication

Two reasons for using authentication for a service are to keep users from doing malicious requests potentially corrupting or deleting your data, and to minimize the load on the data source.

There are four types of authentication you can use for remote data sources:

Basic Username/password authentication; keep in mind that the credentials are **not** encrypted, which means that unauthorized users may get ahold of the credentials.

Digest Username/password authentication where the credentials **are** encrypted.

Windows Windows domain credentials are used to authenticate users and are typically used to provide a single sign-on (SSO) experience.

Certificate The user must have the correct certificate installed to use the service.

The following code sample shows how you can use the **Network-Credential** class to authenticate using **username and password**; we will use this when uploading a file to an FTP site later in this chapter.

```
var request = WebRequest.Create(uri) as FtpWebRequest;

request.Credentials = new NetworkCredential(
   username, password);

request.Method = WebRequestMethods.Ftp.UploadFile;
```

The following code sample shows how you can use the credentials from the currently logged in user; we use the **DefaultCredentials** property of the **CredentialCache** class to get the user credentials.

```
var uri =
"http://school.SourceCodeAcademy.com/SchoolService.svc/
   GetStudentsByLastName";
var request = WebRequest.Create(uri) as HttpWebRequest;

request.Credentials = CredentialCache.DefaultCredentials;
```

The following code sample shows how you can use an **x509Certificate** to authenticate users; by using this type of authentication, the user will automatically gain access if the right certificate is sent with the request. The **GetCertificate** method returns an **X509Certificate2** object that gives the developer access to the x509 certificate.

```
var uri = "http://school.SourceCodeAcademy.com/
       SchoolService.svc/GetStudentsByLastName";
var request = WebRequest.Create(uri) as HttpWebRequest;
var certificate =
   SourceCodeAcademyCertificateServices.GetCertificate();

request.ClientCertificates.Add(certificate);
```

Additional reading: "MSDN NetworkCredential Class"

Create a WCF Data Service

Before we have a look at sending and receiving data from a WCF Data Service, we will have a look at how we can create a new WCF Data Service.

1. In Visual Studio 2012, select **File-New Project** or click the **New Project** link on the start page.
2. In the *New Project* dialog, click the **Web** tab to the left and select **ASP.NET Empty Web Application**.
3. Give the service a name in the **Name** text box and click **OK**.
4. Right click on the project in the **Solution Explorer** and select **Add-New Item**.

5. In the *Add New Item* dialog, click the **Data** tab to the left and select **ADO.NET Entity Data Model** to add a data source and create an EDM for it in the project.
6. Give the EDM a name in the **Name** text box and click **Add**.
7. To connect to an existing data source, select the **Generate from database** option and click **Next**.
8. Select a data source in the drop-down or click **New Connection** to a new connection.
9. Make sure that the correct data source is displayed in the **Data source** field; if not then click Change to change the data source. In the sample code *Microsoft SQL Server (SqlClient)* is used.
10. Select a server in the **Server name** drop-down or specify the server name that you want to use in the drop-down text field. In the sample code, the local SQL Server *(localdb)\v11.0* is used.
11. Select the database you want to use in the **Select or enter a database name** drop-down.
12. Click **Test Connection** to make sure that the connection works.
13. Click **OK**.
14. Give the entity connection settings name in the **Save entity connection settings in Web.Config as** text box. Remember this name because you will use it to reference the data source from the web service class.
15. Click **Next**.
16. Check the database objects you want to create entities for in the list.
17. Give the model namespace a name in the **Model Namespace** text box and click **Finish**. When clicking **Finish,**

an EDM will be created for the database objects you checked, save the EDM.

18. Right click on the project in the **Solution Explorer** and select **Add-New Item**.
19. In the *Add New Item* dialog click the **Web** tab to the left, scroll down and select **WCF Data Service** to add the web service.
20. Give the web service a name in the **Name** text box.
21. The *ServiceName*.svc.cs file opens; this is the web service file that will contain the methods that you want to expose to the consumer. Here you need to add the data source name (from step 14) to the class definition, just replace the comment that shows you where to add the name with the actual name.
22. In the **InitializeService** method you need to add a **SetEntitySetAccessRule** rule to specify how the entities can be used and you also need to add **SetServiceOperationAccessRule** rules for the methods you add to the service; failing to do so will result in that the consumer cannot access the methods. Look at the comments in the method.
23. Add methods to the class and decorate get methods with the [WebGet] attribute and the update methods with the [WebInvoke(Method = "POST")] attribute.
24. Right click on the project in the **Solution Explorer** and select **Properties**.
25. Click the Web tab to the left in the window and make sure that the **Use Local IIS Web Server** and **Use IIS Express** are selected; these setting will assure that the same port is used on subsequent calls. Make a note of the **project URI** you will need it when calling the web service.
26. Save the changes and close the settings window.

You might have to install IIS on your computer by following these steps.

1. Open the *Windows Control Panel.*
2. Click on *Programs and Features*.
3. Click the *Turn Windows features on or off* link
4. Select *Internet Information Services* check box, or drill down into the folder and select what you need to install.
5. Click **OK**; the installation takes a moment.

Read Atom Feed Data

We will look at a couple of ways to parse feed data retrieved using HttpWebRequest and HttpWebResponse instances not setting a reference to the web service in the Solution Explorer.

The Feed Data

We will fetch data about students using a WCF Data Service that returns an *Atom* feed. First let's have a look at what the returned data looks like. The object data is contained within the properties tag so that is the part we will focus on parsing to objects; we will parse using a **DataSet** and an **XmlReader**.

```
<?xml version="1.0" encoding="utf-8"?>
<feed xml:base=
        "http://localhost:56001/WCFSchoolService.svc/"
    xmlns="http://www.w3.org/2005/Atom"
    xmlns:d="http://schemas.microsoft.com/ado/2007/08/
        dataservices"
    xmlns:m="http://schemas.microsoft.com/ado/2007/08/
        dataservices/metadata">
    <id>http://localhost:56001/WCFSchoolService.svc/
        StudentByLastName</id>
    <title type="text">StudentByLastName</title>
    <updated>2013-08-27T12:37:48Z</updated>
    <link rel="self" title="StudentByLastName"
        href="StudentByLastName" />
```

```
    <entry>
        <id>http://localhost:56001/WCFSchoolService.svc/
            Student(4)</id>
        <category term="SchoolDBModel.Student"
            scheme="http://schemas.microsoft.com/ado/
                    2007/08/dataservices/scheme" />
        <link rel="edit" title="Student"
            href="Student(4)" />
        <link
            rel=http://schemas.microsoft.com/ado/2007/08/
                dataservices/related/Teacher
            type="application/atom+xml;type=entry"
            title="Teacher" href="Student(4)/Teacher" />
        <title />
        <updated>2013-08-27T12:37:48Z</updated>
        <author> <name /> </author>
        <content type="application/xml">
            <m:properties>
                <d:Id m:type="Edm.Int32">4</d:Id>
                <d:FirstName>Lisa</d:FirstName>
                <d:LastName>Smith</d:LastName>
                <d:DateOfBirth="" m:type="Edm.DateTime">
                    2005-05-04T00:00:00
                </d:DateOfBirth>
                <d:ClassId
                    m:type="Edm.Int32">1</d:ClassId>
            </m:properties>
        </content>
    </entry>
</feed>
```

Reading an Atom Feed using a DataSet

We can parse using the **ReadXml** method on a **DataSet** instance and looping through the table rows. We fill the data set by passing the response stream to the **ReadXml** method. You have to look in the **DataSet** instance to see what tables are available; it can differ with different data sources.

```
public List<WCFPerson> ParseFeedUsingDataSet(string uri)
{
    // Contains the finished objects
    List<WCFPerson> paresedObjects =
        new List<WCFPerson>();

    // Get the RSS feed using a HttpWebRequest
    HttpWebRequest rssFeed =
        (HttpWebRequest)WebRequest.Create(uri);

    var response = rssFeed.GetResponse() as
        HttpWebResponse;

    //use a dataset to retrieve the RSS feed
    using (DataSet rssData = new DataSet())
    {
        //Parse the feed from XML to data tables
        rssData.ReadXml(
            rssFeed.GetResponse().GetResponseStream());

        // Loop over RSS entries and create a list
        for (int i = 0; i <
        rssData.Tables["properties"].Rows.Count; i++)
        {
            var name =
                rssData.Tables["properties"].Rows[i];
            var classId =
                rssData.Tables["ClassId"].Rows[i];
            var id = rssData.Tables["Id"].Rows[i];
            var dob =
                rssData.Tables["DateofBirth"].Rows[i];

            paresedObjects.Add(new WCFPerson
            {
                Id = Convert.ToInt32(id[1]),
                FirstName = Convert.ToString(name[1]),
                LastName = Convert.ToString(name[2]),
                DateOfBirth = Convert.ToDateTime(dob[1]),
                ClassId = Convert.ToInt32(classId[1])
            });
        }
    }
```

```
    return paresedObjects;
}

private void ReadFromWebServiceWithoutReference()
{
    List<WCFPerson> students =
        ParseFeedUsingDataSet(webServiceUri +
            "StudentByLastName?lastName='Smith'");
}
```

Reading an Atom Feed using an XmlReader

We can parse using the XmlReader. The parsing method that we use is declared as async Task<List<WCFPerson>> which means that the run asynchronously and returns a list of **WCFPerson** objects.

Before we can call the **Create** method on the XmlReader instance, we need to create an instance of the **XmlReaderSettings** class and set the **Async** property to true to enable reading asynchronously from the service. We pass this object to the **Create** method when calling the web service.

In the while declaration, we use the **ReadAsync** method on the **XmlReader** instance to fetch the next node in the stream; note that the call is declared with the **await** keyword to process each node in an asynchronous stream.

Within the while loop, we use a switch that checks if the element is a starting element, text or an end element. If it is a starting element, we check if the node name is equal to **"m:properties"** which is when a new object needs to be created because that signifies a new segment of student values. We also check if the name starts with ":d" because that signifies a property; if it does, then we save the value in a temporary variable that will be used when we reach the end element.

If the element is text, then we store that value in a temporary variable that is used in the end element to save it to correct property in the student object.

When we reach the end element, we check that the element name is equal to the stored property name; if it is then we store the value in the property with the same name as the element and we reset the temporary variable holding the property name. We also check if the element name is **“m:properties”** which means that we have reached the end of the student data for the current student.

In order to set the property value dynamically, we use reflection. The **GetProperty** method called on a type will return with the specified name if it exists otherwise it returns null. The **SetValue** method on the property instance can be used to set the value of the passed-in object (the student instance); to be able to set the value we need to pass in the correct type to cast the value to the correct data type. To pass in the correct data type, we use the **ChangeType** method on the **Convert** class.

```
async Task<List<WCFPerson>> CreateAndFillObjects(Stream
stream)
{
    List<WCFPerson> paresedObjects =
        new List<WCFPerson>();
    WCFPerson student = null;
    object value = null;
    string startElenmentName = String.Empty;

    XmlReaderSettings settings = new XmlReaderSettings();
    settings.Async = true;

    using (XmlReader reader = XmlReader.Create(
    stream, settings))
    {
        while (await reader.ReadAsync())
        {
            switch (reader.NodeType)
            {
                case XmlNodeType.Element:
                    if (reader.Name == "m:properties")
                        student = new WCFPerson();
```

```
                    if (reader.Name.StartsWith("d:"))
                        startElenmentName =
                            reader.Name.Substring(2);
                    break;
                case XmlNodeType.Text:
                    value = await reader.GetValueAsync();
                    break;
                case XmlNodeType.EndElement:
                    if (reader.Name.StartsWith("d:") &&
                    startElenmentName ==
                    reader.Name.Substring(2))
                    {
                        var property = student.GetType()
                        .GetProperty(startElenmentName);

                        if (property != null &&
                        student != null)
                            property.SetValue(student,
                                Convert.ChangeType(value,
                                property.PropertyType));

                            startElenmentName =
                                String.Empty;
                    }
                        if (reader.Name == "m:properties"
                        && student != null)
                            paresedObjects.Add(student);
                break;
            }
        }
    }
    return paresedObjects;
}
```

When calling the **CreateAndFillObjects** method, we pass in a stream that we have fetched using a WCF Data Service using **HttpWebRequest** and **HttpResponse** objects, and the URI to the web service.

We return the list of students using the Result property on the Task <List<WCFPerson>> that is returned from the asynchronous function.

```
private List<WCFPerson> ParseFeedUsingXmlReader(
string uri)
{
    HttpWebRequest rssFeed =
        (HttpWebRequest)WebRequest.Create(uri);

    var response = rssFeed.GetResponse() as
        HttpWebResponse;

    return CreateAndFillObjects(
        response.GetResponseStream()).Result;
}

private void ReadFromWebServiceWithoutReference()
{
    List<WCFPerson> students2 =
        ParseFeedUsingXmlReader(webServiceUri +
            "StudentByLastName?lastName='Smith'");
}
```

Additional reading: "MSDN LINQ to XML"

Update Data

We will look at how we can send data to a WCF Data Service to update the data source using **HttpWebRequest** and **HttpWebResponse** objects as well as with a service reference and an entity context object.

Adding Data Without Using a Service Reference

When we do not have a service reference to rely on we can use **HttpWebRequest** and **HttpWebResponse** objects to update data in the data source. Apart from creating an **HttpWebRequest** instance using the **WebRequest** class we need to remember to set the **Method** property to **POST** and the **ContentLength** to **zero** for the request object before we call the **GetResponse** method; failing to set these two properties will result in an exception being thrown. Even though we don't have any data to attach to the request we need to specify the **ContentLength**. The values will be sent in through the URI combined with the web service location and the method name.

The base URI could be:

http://localhost:56001/WCFSchoolService.svc/AddStudent

and the parameters could be:

?firstName='Jonas'&lastName='Fagerberg'&classId='1'
&dob='1970-05-04'.

```
public void SendData(string uri, string parameters)
{
    HttpWebRequest request =
        (HttpWebRequest)WebRequest.Create(
            uri + parameters);

    request.Method = "POST";
    request.ContentLength = 0;

    HttpWebResponse response =
        (HttpWebResponse)request.GetResponse();
}
```

To call the SendData method, we need to pass in the URI to the **AddStudent** function along with the values from a student object; note that the **UriParameters** property defined in the **WCFPerson** class returns a string formatted to suit the needs of a HTTP parameter list.

We are not actually passing in the **WCFPerson** object, just the values formatted as a URL parameter list.

```
private void WriteToWebServiceWithoutReference()
{
    SendData(webServiceUri + "AddStudent", new WCFPerson()
    {
        FirstName = "Jonas",
        LastName = "Fagerberg",
        DateOfBirth = new DateTime(1970, 5, 4),
        ClassId = 1
    }.UriParameters);
}
```

Uploading to an FTP Site

To upload a file to an FTP site, we use an **FtpWebRequest** instance and the File class to read the data stored in the file.

In order to get access to the FTP site, we need to send credentials with the request, we assign a **NetworkCredential** object to the **Credentials** property on the request instance to achieve this.

In order for the request to know what to do with the data, we need to set the **Method** property on the request object; in our case, we set it to **UploadFile** since that is what we intend to do.

The request object also needs to know the size of the data that is being streamed to the FTP site.

Now that we are ready to stream our data, we get a request stream that we can write the data to using the **GetRequestStream** method on the request object. The last thing we do is to write the file data buffer to the stream and close the stream when it has finished.

```
private void UploadToFTP(string filePathOnDrive, string
uri, string username, string password)
{
    var fileData = File.ReadAllBytes(filePathOnDrive);

    var request = WebRequest.Create(uri) as FtpWebRequest;
    request.Credentials = new NetworkCredential(
        username, password);
    request.Method = WebRequestMethods.Ftp.UploadFile;
    request.ContentLength = fileData.Length;

    var dataStream = request.GetRequestStream();
    dataStream.Write(fileData, 0, fileData.Length);
    dataStream.Close();
}
```

Cloud Data and REST Services

WCF Data Service can be easily accessed from many different types of client applications. Because WCF Data Services follows the *Representational State Transfer (REST)* architectural model and open web standards such as *Open Data Protocol (OData)* they can be used regardless of what technology is used to build the client application.

The REST model support HTTP, GET, PUT, POST and DELETE requests; it also support filtering of the data. You also can write your own methods that you can call over the HTTP protocol.

In a WCF Data Service, the entities in an *Entity Data Model (EDM)* can be accessed through the URI directly in a browser. The returned data can be formatted in well-known formats such as XML and Atom; this means that data is returned in collections that are supported by REST.

By default, WCF Data Services do not expose any resources such as the EDM objects, you have to manually set these privileges in the **InitializeService** method calling the **config.SetEntitySetAccessRule** method; to specify all resources use an asterisk (*) for the first parameter. The second parameter, **EntitySetRights,** sets the access to the resource.

The **config.MaxProtocolVersion** property sets the maximum protocol version that this service response supports.

The **config.SetServiceOperationAccessRule** is used to define the custom methods that are created in the service; you must define then here to expose them outside the service, the **ServiceOperationRights** parameter set the access rights to the method outside the service.

```
Public static void
InitializeService(DataServiceConfiguration config)
{
    config.SetEntitySetAccessRule("*",
EntitySetRights.All);
    config.DataServiceBehavior.MaxProtocolVersion =
DataServiceProtocolVersion.V3;
    config.SetServiceOperationAccessRule("StudentsByLastNa
me", ServiceOperationRights.All);
}
```

REST is well-suited to represent resources and business objects over a network because it describes a stateless, hierarchical scheme. Data is accessed through the service URI and the exposed entities; for instance **http://localhost:7907/WCFSchoolRestDataService.svc/Students** would fetch all students and **http://localhost:7907/WCFSchoolRestData-Service.svc/Students?$top=3** would fetch the first three students in the data source.

http://localhost:7907/WCFSchoolRestDataService.svc/Students(2) would fetch the student with id 2. Because there is a relation between the Student and Teacher, tables the following URI will fetch the teacher for the student with id 2. **http://localhost:7907/WCFSchoolRestData-Service.svc/ Students(2)/Teacher**.

It is up to the organization or company to decide the exact URI pattern that will be used to expose data through the web service.

WCF Data Services can expose non-relational data but that requires customized classes.

Additional reading:"How to: Add, Modify, and Delete Entities (WCF Data Services)" and "WCF Data Services 4.5"

Create a WCF REST Data Service

WCF Data Services are built on the generic **System.Data.Services.DaraService** class; they require that its type parameter is satisfied by an **IEnumerable<T>** or an **IQueryable<T>** interface such as **DbContext** that the WCF Data Service class inherits. The basic functionality to expose entities in the collection as REST resources are implemented by the **DataService** parameter; if you want, you can override methods in the **DataService** class to build custom functionality.

Methods that return data must be decorated with the **WebGet** attribute and methods that accessed through POST, PUT or DELETE must be decorated with the **WebInvoke** attribute. Methods that you create do not have to return data although they usually do. A method that returns a single value should be decorated with the **[SingleResult]** attribute.

A *WCF REST Data Service* is a *WCF Data Service* that uses the *Representational Sate Transfer (REST)* architectural model when communicating.

You can read how to create a WCF Data Service in the Create a WCF Data Service section. The sample uses the name *WCFSchoolRestDataService* for the WCF Data Service.

We want to use a data source to return data from a Microsoft SQL Server database; you can read how to add an Entity Data Model to a project in the Create an EDM from an Existing Database section. The sample uses the name *SchoolModel* for the EDM and *SchoolDBEntities* for the entity connection; the latter class is used to create the data source context that connects to the data source.

Additional reading: ”Service Operations (WCF Data Services)”aand ”Exposing Your Data as a Service (WCF Data Services)”

Reference a Web Service from the Client Application

1. Right-clicking on the **References** folder and select **Add Service Reference**.

2. Click on the **Discover** button (or write the URI to the service in the text field and click the **GO** button if it is a remote service that is not in the solution).

3. Select the web service in the list, give it a namespace name and click **OK**.

Additional reading: "WCF Data Service Client Utility (DataSvcUtil.exe)"

Read Data from a WCF REST Data Service

We will have a look at how we can read data using the context object and custom web service methods.

The following context object will be used to manipulate data in the upcoming samples.

```
class Program
{
    private const string restServiceUri =
    "http://localhost:7907/WCFSchoolRestDataService.svc/";

    private static WCFRestDataSchoolServiceReference
        .SchoolDBEntities Context;

    static void Main(string[] args)
    {
        Context = new WCFRestDataSchoolServiceReference
            .SchoolDBEntities(new Uri(restServiceUri));
    }
}
```

Reading Data Using the Context Object from the Client

An easy way to call a WCF Data Service is to add a reference to the service in the **Solution Explorer**. To set a reference to a web service you right click on the **References** folder in the **Solution Explorer** and select **Add-Service Reference**; in the *Add Reference* dialog you click the **Discover** button if the web service is in the same solution, otherwise you type in the URI to the web service in the text field and click the **Go** button. Select the web service in the list, give it a name and click **OK**; the name you specify will be the namespace you use when referencing the web service from the code.

To create a context, or proxy, to the web service you create an instance of the **DbContext** class in the EDM in the service, the name usually ends with *Entities*; pass in the base URI to the web service in constructor. You then use the desired entities (tables) on the context instance to fetch data; using LINQ makes it really easy to fetch and manipulate the data.

Using the context object

The following sample code shows how you can use the entity on the web service context object directly from the client when fetching data.

```
public static IQueryable<Student>
GetStudentsByLastName(string lastName)
{
    IQueryable<Student> students =
        from s in Context.Students
        where s.LastName == lastName
        select s;

    return students;
}
```

The following sample code shows how you can call a custom web service method to fetch data.

The web service method

```
[WebGet(UriTemplate =
"StudentsByLastName?lastName={lastName}")]
public IQueryable<Student> StudentsByLastName(
string lastName)
{
    if (!String.IsNullOrEmpty(lastName))
    {
        return
            from s in this.CurrentDataSource.Students
            where String.Equals(s.LastName, lastName)
            select s;
    }
    else
    {
        throw new ArgumentException(
            "Last name must be specified.", "lastName");
    }
}
```

The client call

```
public static IEnumerable<Student>
GetStudentsByLastName(string lastName)
{
    return
        from student in Context.Execute<Student>
        (
            new Uri(String.Format(
                "/StudentsByLastName?lastName='{0}'",
                lastName),
            UriKind.Relative)
        )
        where student.LastName == lastName
        select student;
}
```

Eager Loading

Eager loading is beneficial if you know that you need related entities to the one you fetch, just beware that it can have negative impact on bandwidth. You use the Expand method to implement eager loading. By default, related entities are not loaded.

```
public IQueryable<Student>
GetStudentsByLastNameEagerLoading(string lastName)
{
    IQueryable<Student> students =
        from s in Context.Students.Expand("Teacher")
        where s.LastName == lastName
        select s;

    return students;
}
```

Explicit Loading

This is similar to eager loading with the difference being that fetching the related entity is done on demand when it is needed, saving bandwidth; using the **LoadProperty** method on the context object.

```
public static void GetStudentsByLastNameExplicitLoading()
{
    foreach (var student in Context.Students)
    {
        Context.LoadProperty(student, "Teacher");
        Console.WriteLine(String.Format(
            "Student: {0, -10}{1,-15} " +
            "Teacher: {2, -10}{3, -10}",
            student.FirstName, student.LastName,
            student.Teacher.FirstName,
            student.Teacher.LastName));
    }
}
```

Modify data with a WCF REST Data Service

We will look at how we can add, update and delete data using the context object and custom methods.

We will look at how we can send data to a WCF Data Service to update student information using a service reference and an entity context object. When creating the context object, we need to pass in the URI to the web service in the constructor.

The first thing we need to do is to create the context object, a proxy, to the entity object in the WCF Data Service Reference; we will use this context object to modify the student data.

Update data

To fetch the correct student, we use LINQ to query the **Student** table in the data source using the student ID as a filter. Then we set the properties to the values of the properties in the **Student** object passed-in.

Using the context object

The following sample code shows how you can use the entity on the web service context object directly from the client when updating data.

To save the values, we need to call two methods on the context object, **UpdateObject** to save the changes to the client model data and **SaveChanges** to persist the data to the data source through the web service.

```
public static void UpdateStudent(Student student)
 {
    var selectedStudent =
        (
            from s in Context.Students
            where s.Id.Equals(student.Id)
            select s
        ).Single();

    selectedStudent.FirstName = student.FirstName;
    selectedStudent.LastName = student.LastName;
    selectedStudent.ClassId = student.ClassId;
    selectedStudent.DateOfBirth = student.DateOfBirth;

    Context.UpdateObject(selectedStudent);
    Context.SaveChanges();
 }
```

The following sample code shows how you can call a custom web service method to update data. Do not forget to call the SaveChanges method on the CurrentDataSource instance or else the data will not be persisted.

The web service method

```
[WebInvoke(Method = "POST", UriTemplate =
"UpdateStudent?id={id}&firstName={firstName}&lastName=
{lastName}&classId={classId}&dob={dob}")]
public void UpdateStudent(string id, string firstName,
string lastName, string classId, string dob)
{
   int studentId = Convert.ToInt32(id);
   int clsId = Convert.ToInt32(classId);
   DateTime dataOfBirth = Convert.ToDateTime(dob);

   if (studentId > 0 &&
       !String.IsNullOrEmpty(firstName) &&
       !String.IsNullOrEmpty(lastName) &&
       clsId > 0 && !dob.Equals(DateTime.MinValue))
   {
       var student = (
           from s in CurrentDataSource.Students
           where s.Id.Equals(studentId)
           select s).Single();

       student.FirstName = firstName;
       student.LastName = lastName;
       student.ClassId = clsId;
       student.DateOfBirth = dataOfBirth;

       CurrentDataSource.SaveChanges();
   }
   else
   {
       throw new ArgumentException(
           "Missing information.", "");
   }
}
```

The client call

```
public static void UpdateStudent(Student student)
{
    Context.Execute(new Uri(String.Format(
        "/UpdateStudent{0}",
        student.GetUpdateUriParameters()),
        UriKind.Relative), "POST", null);
}
```

Add data

To fetch the correct student, we use LINQ to query the **Student** table in the data source using the student ID as a filter. Then we set the properties to the values of the properties in the **Student** object passed-in.

Using the context object

The following sample code shows how you can use the entity on the web service context object directly from the client when adding data.

To save the values, we need to call two methods on the context object: **AddObject** to save the changes to the client model data and **SaveChanges** to persist the data to the data source through the web service.

```
public static void AddStudent(Student student)
{
    Context.AddObject("Students", student);
    Context.SaveChanges();
}
```

The following sample code shows how you can call a custom web service method to add data. Do not forget to call the **SaveChanges** method on the **CurrentDataSource** instance or else the data will not be persisted.

The web service method

```
[WebInvoke(Method = "POST", UriTemplate =
"AddStudent?firstName={firstName}&lastName=
{lastName}&classId={classId}&dob={dob}")]
public void AddStudent(string firstName, string lastName,
string classId, string dob)
{
   if (!String.IsNullOrEmpty(firstName) &&
       !String.IsNullOrEmpty(lastName) &&
       !String.IsNullOrEmpty(classId) &&
       !String.IsNullOrEmpty(dob))
   {
       this.CurrentDataSource.Students.Add(new Student
       {
           FirstName = firstName,
           LastName = lastName,
           ClassId = Convert.ToInt32(classId),
           DateOfBirth = Convert.ToDateTime(dob)
       });

       this.CurrentDataSource.SaveChanges();
   }
   else
   {
       throw new ArgumentException(
           "Missing information.", "");
   }
}
```

The client call

```
public static void AddStudent(Student student)
{
   Context.Execute(new Uri(String.Format(
       "/AddStudent{0}", student.GetAddUriParameters()),
       UriKind.Relative), "POST", null);
}
```

Delete data

To fetch the correct student, we use LINQ to query the **Student** table in the data source using the passed-in student id as a filter.

Using the context object

The following sample code shows how you can use the entity on the web service context object directly from the client when deleting data.

To save the values, we need to call two methods on the context object: **DeleteObject** to save the changes to the client model data and **SaveChanges** to persist the data to the data source through the web service.

```
public static void DeleteStudent(int id)
{
    if (id > 0)
    {
        var student =
            (
                from s in Context.Students
                where s.Id.Equals(id)
                select s
            ).Single();

        Context.DeleteObject(student);
        Context.SaveChanges();
    }
    else
    {
        throw new ArgumentException(
            "Missing information.", "");
    }
}
```

The following sample code shows how you can call a custom web service method to deleting data. Do not forget to call the **SaveChanges** method on the **CurrentDataSource** instance or else the data will not be persisted.

The web service method

```
[WebInvoke(Method = "POST", UriTemplate =
"DeleteStudent?id={id}")]
public void DeleteStudent(string id)
{
   int studentId = Convert.ToInt32(id);

   if (studentId > 0)
   {
       var student =
           (
               from s in CurrentDataSource.Students
               where s.Id.Equals(studentId)
               select s
           ).Single();

       CurrentDataSource.Students.Remove(student);
       CurrentDataSource.SaveChanges();
   }
   else
   {
       throw new ArgumentException(
           "Missing information.", "");
   }
}
```

The client call

```
public static void DeleteStudent(int studentId)
{
   Context.Execute(new Uri(String.Format(
       "/DeleteStudent?id='{0}'",
       studentId.ToString()), UriKind.Relative),
       "POST", null);
}
```

XAML User Interface

A WPF application is created using XAML to define the User Interface (UI); when the code is compiled, the build engine will create classes and controls from the XAML hierarchy.

XAML is very similar to XML and uses a hierarchical way to define a UI; many developers prefer to work only with XAML and close the design view.

Common Controls

You can add controls in three ways: You can double click on a control in the Toolbox, drag a control from the toolbox to the design surface, or write the XAML code for the control in the XAML window. The default way to view the windows that you create is to have a split view where the design view is on top and the XAML cod at the bottom; you can change this view using the tabs and buttons on the separator bar.

When starting a project, a window is created and displayed for you, the only thing you have to do is to start designing the UI. You can, of course, add windows to the UI whenever the need arises by right-clicking on the project in the Solution Explorer and selecting **Add-Window**.

The window is a container that can contain controls and be displayed as part of the UI; by default, the **Window** element contains a **Grid** control that helps organize the intrinsic controls in the window. The grid control can be customized to hold many rows and columns; by default, it holds one row and one column. You can then place a grid or another layout control nested within the first **Grid** control.

You can assign values to attributes within the **Window** element; typical attributes that are used are **Height**, **Width** and **Title**.

The following sample code shows the default layout of a window when added to the project.

```
<Window x:Class="XAML_Controls.MainWindow"
    xmlns="http://schemas.microsoft.com/winfx/2006/
        xaml/presentation"
    xmlns:x="http://schemas.microsoft.com/winfx/
        2006/xaml"
    Title="MainWindow" Height="350" Width="525">
    <Grid>

    </Grid>
</Window>
```

When creating a UI, you can use the already built-in .NET Framework controls or create your own custom-built user controls.

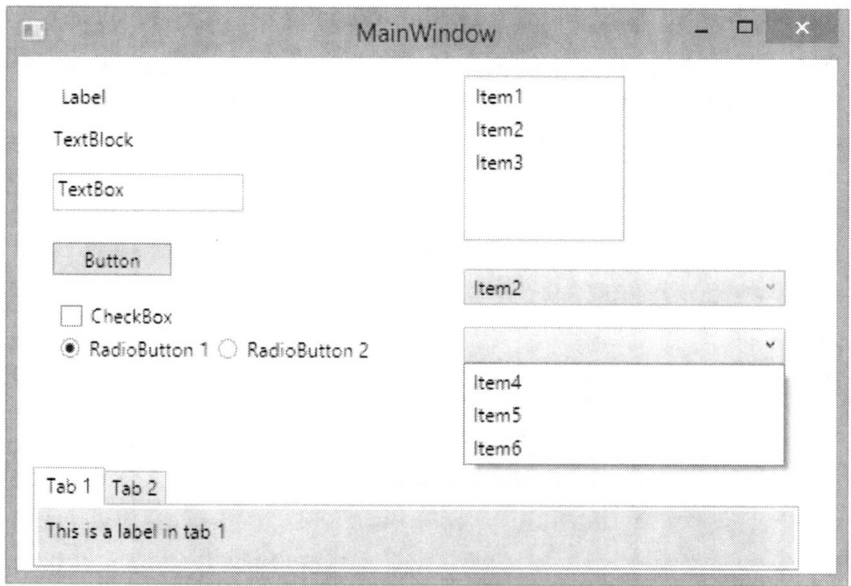

Image 19-1: Common XAML Controls

Control Properties

When adding a control, you generally want to customize it by setting properties on it; you can set properties using XAML in two ways, either by assigning values to its attributes or adding property elements. If the need arises, you also can set properties from the **Window** code behind file using C#; you use this method of setting property values if the values have to change during run-time.

This sample code shows how you can create a gradient background using property elements and property attributes to set the **Width** and **Content**.

Image 19-2: Button Background

```
<Button Content="Button with background"
   HorizontalAlignment="Left" Margin="111,112,0,0"
   VerticalAlignment="Top" Width="162">
   <Button.Background>
       <LinearGradientBrush StartPoint="0.5, 0.5"
           EndPoint="1.5, 1.5" >
           <GradientStop Color="LightBlue" Offset="0" />
           <GradientStop Color="Blue" Offset="0.75" />
       </LinearGradientBrush>
   </Button.Background>

   <Button.Foreground>
       <SolidColorBrush Color="Black" />
   </Button.Foreground>
</Button>
```

The following code sample shows how you can set the content property on a button and a label using C# code in the **Window** code behind file to change the displayed text in those controls.

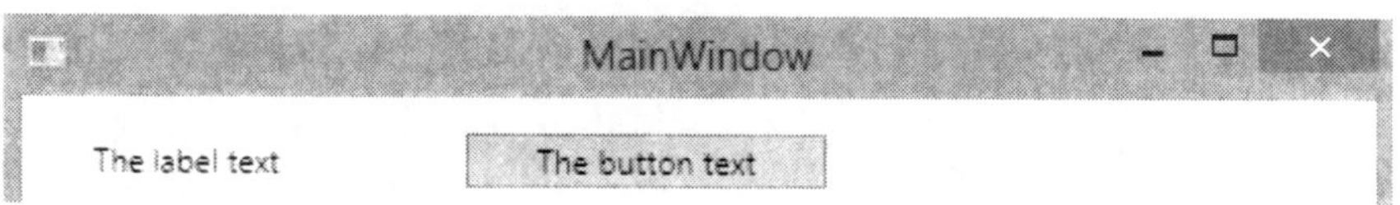

Image 19-3: Button and Label

```
Button1.Content = "The button text";
Label1.Content = "The label text";
```

Frequently Used Properties

Property	Description
Name	The name of the control; can be used to reference the control from the code behind.
Content	The text or intrinsic controls stored in the control.
Horizontal-Alignment	The horizontal alignment of the control.
Vertical-Alignment	The vertical alignment of the control.
Margin= "L,T,R,B"	The margin surrounding the control; the values are specified in the following order: left, top, right, bottom.
Text-Wrapping	Specifies whether or not the text in the control will be wrapped to the next line if the text is longer than the text area size.
Text	This property contains the text of text control such as TextBox and TextBlock.
Width	Specifies the width of the control.
Height	Specifies the height of the control.

Property	Description
GroupName	For grouped controls such as RadioButton this is the name that binds them together and makes them work as a unit.
IsChecked	Can be used to check if a checkable control such as RadioButton or CheckBox is checked or not.

Label

A label is a control that displays a static or non-editable single row of text; it is usually added to denote what other controls are used for or contain such as First name or Last name for a **TextBox** control.

```
<Label Name="Label1" Content="The label text"
HorizontalAlignment="Left" VerticalAlignment="Top"
Margin="22,10,0,0"/>
```

C# sample

```
Label1.Content = "The label text";
```

TextBlock

This is a lightweight control for displaying small amounts of text or flow content.

```
<TextBlock Name="TextBlock1" HorizontalAlignment="Left"
TextWrapping="Wrap" VerticalAlignment="Top"
Margin="22,41,0,0" Text="The TextBlock text goes here."/>
```

C# sample

```
TextBlock1.Text = "The textblock text goes here.";
```

TextBox

This control is used to collect text input from the user such as First name or Last name.

```
<TextBox Name="TextBox1" HorizontalAlignment="Left"
Height="23" TextWrapping="Wrap" Text="Text box text"
VerticalAlignment="Top" Width="120" Margin="22,70,0,0"/>
```

C# sample – Shows how to write a value in a **TextBox** control and retrieve the value and convert it.

```
TextBox1.Text = "100";
var theTextBoxValue = Convert.ToInt32(TextBox1.Text);
```

Control Events

Controls have events that can be implemented as methods to open up for interaction or handle system events. There is, for instance, an event that handles button clicks; if you want code to be executed when a user clicks a specific button, you need to link an event handler method that button's click event. Other scenarios are handling clicks in **ListBox** and **ComboBox** controls or hovering over a control.

Vent code is handled by the code behind (.cs) file for the window or user-defined control: you can declare the connection between event and event handler method in XAML or with C# in the code behind.

WPF uses the concept of ***routed events,*** which means that it will search for an event in the current control and if it does not find a suitable event there, it bubbles up the event to the parent control; this can be useful if you want to implement a default event handler for vents that are not handled by the intrinsic controls themselves. Even if the child control handles an event, the event is still bubbled to the parent control in case it needs to do some processing. The *RoutedEventArgs* parameter of the event contains information about the event; it also contain a property called **Handled** that indicates whether the event already has been handled, you can set this property to tell the parent event handler that the event already has been handled.

The easiest way to implement an event handler method is to double-click the control, just make sure it is not already selected and that you do not double-click on the text or intrinsic controls of the control.

Additional reading: "Routed Events Overview"

Specific implementation examples can be read under respective control section.

This sample shows how you can define an event using XAML.

```
<Button Name="Button1" Content="Button"
HorizontalAlignment="Left" VerticalAlignment="Top"
Width="98" Margin="22,112,0,0" Click="Button1_Click"/>
```

```
private void Button1_Click(object sender,
RoutedEventArgs e)
{
    Label1.Content = "The label text";
}
```

This sample shows how you can define an event in the initialization method of the window using C#.

```
<Button Name="Button2" Content="Button"
HorizontalAlignment="Left" VerticalAlignment="Top"
Width="98" Margin="22,112,0,0"/>
```

```
public MainWindow()
{
    Button2.Click += Button2_Click;
}
private void Button2_Click(object sender,
RoutedEventArgs e)
{
    Label1.Content = "The label text";
}
```

Button

The button is used to enable the user to perform a specific action; to handle the click event that is raised when a user clicks the button you need to create an event method in the code behind.

```
<Button Name="Button1" Content="Button"
HorizontalAlignment="Left" VerticalAlignment="Top"
Width="98" Margin="22,112,0,0" Click="Button1_Click"/>
```

```
private void Button1_Click(object sender,
RoutedEventArgs e)
{
    Label1.Content = "The label text";
}
```

Checkbox

The checkbox control is used to indicate that something is selected or not selected. To find out if the checkbox is checked you use the **IsChecked** property of the checkbox control. If you want to perform a task when the user clicks the checkbox, then you implement the **Click** event of the checkbox. If you want to perform a task when the checkbox is checked, then implement the **Checked** event of the checkbox. If you want to perform a task when the checkbox is unchecked, then implement the **Unchecked** event of the checkbox.

```
<CheckBox Name="CheckBox1" Content="CheckBox"
HorizontalAlignment="Left" VerticalAlignment="Top"
Margin="26,149,0,0" Click="CheckBox1_Click"
Checked="CheckBox1_Checked"
Unchecked="CheckBox1_Unchecked"/>
```

```
private void CheckBox1_Click(object sender,
RoutedEventArgs e)
{
    Label1.Content = "Checkbox clicked";
}
```

```
private void CheckBox1_Checked(object sender,
RoutedEventArgs e)
{
    Label1.Content = "Checkbox checked";
}

private void CheckBox1_Unchecked(object sender,
RoutedEventArgs e)
{
    Label1.Content = "Checkbox unchecked";
}
```

RadioButton

The radio button control is used to present the user with a multiple choice option where only one of the values can be selected. Use the **GroupName** property to specify which radio button controls that belongs to a certain group of radio buttons; this is necessary to distinguish different groups of radio button controls.

To find out if a radio button is checked, use the **IsChecked** property.

If you want to perform a task when the user clicks the radio button, implement the **Click** event of the radio button. If you want to perform a task when the radio button is checked, then implement the **Checked** event of the radio button. If you want to perform a task when the radio button is unchecked, then implement the **Unchecked** event of the radio button. You can connect several radio buttons to the same event handler if you want to perform the same task when one of them gets clicked or selected.

In the sample code, we have connected both the radio buttons' events to the same event handler methods. Note also that we use the **e.Source** property to get the name of the control that raised the event.

```
<RadioButton Name="RB1" Content="RadioButton 1"
HorizontalAlignment="Left" VerticalAlignment="Top"
Margin="26,169,0,0" GroupName="RBGroup" IsChecked="True"
Click="RadioButton_Click" Checked="RadioButton_Checked"
Unchecked="RadioButton_Unchecked"/>

<RadioButton Name="RB2" Content="RadioButton 2"
HorizontalAlignment="Left" VerticalAlignment="Top"
Margin="125,169,0,0" GroupName="RBGroup"
Click="RadioButton_Click" Checked="RadioButton_Checked"
Unchecked="RadioButton_Unchecked"/>
```

```
private void RadioButton_Click(object sender,
RoutedEventArgs e)
{
   Label1.Content = String.Format(
       "Radio button {0} was clicked",
       ((RadioButton)e.Source).Name);
}

private void RadioButton_Checked(object sender,
RoutedEventArgs e)
{
   Label1.Content = String.Format(
       "Radio button {0} was checked",
       ((RadioButton)e.Source).Name);
}

private void RadioButton_Unchecked(object sender,
RoutedEventArgs e)
{
   Label1.Content = String.Format(
       "Radio button {0} was unchecked",
       ((RadioButton)e.Source).Name);
}
```

ComboBox

The **ComboBox** control is used to present a drop-down list of choices to the user. The items in the list can be added manually with XAML or C# code, or the **ItemSource** property can be set to a collection of values.

Use the **SelectionChanged** event to execute code when an item in the drop-down list has been selected and the **SelectedIndex**, **SelectedItem** and **SelectedValue** properties to use the value or index of the selected item.

The following sample code shows how to add items manually using XAML.

```
<ComboBox Text="Combobox is not open"
HorizontalAlignment="Left" VerticalAlignment="Top"
Width="200" Margin="308,162,0,0"
SelectionChanged="ComboBox_SelectionChanged">
    <ComboBoxItem Name="item1">Item1</ComboBoxItem>
    <ComboBoxItem Name="item2">Item2</ComboBoxItem>
    <ComboBoxItem Name="item3">Item3</ComboBoxItem>
</ComboBox>
```

The following sample code shows how to add items using the **Item-Source** property with C#.

```
List<string> values = new List<string>()
    { "value 1", "value 2", "value 3" };

Combo1.ItemsSource = values;
```

The following sample code shows how to implement the **SelectionChanged** event handler method in the code behind.

```
private void ComboBox_SelectionChanged(object sender,
SelectionChangedEventArgs e)
{
    var index = ((ComboBox)e.Source).SelectedIndex;
    var value = ((ComboBox)e.Source).SelectedValue;
    var item = ((ComboBox)e.Source).SelectedItem;
}
```

ListBox

The list box control is used to present a list of choices to the user. The items in the list can be added manually with XAML or C# code, or the **ItemSource** property can be set to a collection of values.

Use the **SelectionChanged** event to execute code when an item in the list has been selected and the **SelectedIndex**, **SelectedItem** and **SelectedValue** properties to use the value or index of the selected item.

The following sample code shows how to add items manually using XAML.

```
<ListBox Name="List1" HorizontalAlignment="Left"
Height="100" VerticalAlignment="Top" Width="100"
Margin="308,10,0,0"
SelectionChanged="ListBox_SelectionChanged">
    <ListBoxItem Name="Item1">Item1</ListBoxItem>
    <ListBoxItem Name="Item2">Item2</ListBoxItem>
    <ListBoxItem Name="Item3">Item3</ListBoxItem>
</ListBox>
```

The following sample code shows how to add items using the **Item-Source** property with C#.

```
List<string> values = new List<string>()
    { "value 1", "value 2", "value 3" };

List1.ItemsSource = values;
```

The following sample code shows how to implement the **Selection-Changed** event handler method in the code behind.

```
private void ListBox_SelectionChanged(object sender,
SelectionChangedEventArgs e)
{
    var index = ((ListBox)e.Source).SelectedIndex;
    var value = ((ListBox)e.Source).SelectedValue;
    var item = ((ListBox)e.Source).SelectedItem;
}
```

TabControl

The tab control presents "pages" that the user can click to view information and controls related to a specific topic that the tab has.

To add controls to a tab, click the tab in the designer and place controls in the area below the tab, or add the controls using XAML.

Usually you do not have to create event handlers for the tabs or the tab container because it handles hiding and showing the tab pages automatically as they are clicked.

The following sample code shows how to add a tab control using XAML.

```
<TabControl HorizontalAlignment="Left" Height="61"
VerticalAlignment="Top" Width="477" Margin="10,248,0,0">
    <TabItem Header="Tab 1">
        <Grid Background="#FFE5E5E5">
            <Label Content="This is a label in tab 1"
                HorizontalAlignment="Left"
                VerticalAlignment="Top"/>
        </Grid>
    </TabItem>
    <TabItem Header="Tab 2">
        <Grid Background="#FFE5E5E5">
            <Label Content="This is a label in tab 2"
                HorizontalAlignment="Left"
                VerticalAlignment="Top"/>
        </Grid>
    </TabItem>
</TabControl>
```

Layout Controls

Layout in WPF has a core principle and that is that the window should render correctly no matter how the user resizes or positions the application window; this is achieved by using relative positioning.

There are several layout or container controls that you can use to position and resize intrinsic controls such as **Grid**, **DockPanel**, **Canvas** and **WrapPanel**.

Grid

A grid layout with columns and rows is used to place the intrinsic controls; use the **RowDefinition** and **ColumnDefinition** elements of the **Grid** to specify the height, width and number of rows and columns the **Grid** control should have.

When placing controls in the **Grid** you use the **Grid.Row** and **Grid.Column** attributes of the child control.

There are three ways you can specify height and width:

1. **Width = "100"** will set the width to 100 units (where 1 unit is 1/96th of an inch).
2. **Width = "Auto"** Will set the width to the smallest width required to render the intrinsic controls.
3. **Width = "*"** Will use up the remaining space after the fixed and auto-width columns are allocated. If more than one column width is specified using an asterisk, (*) then they split the remaining space at a ration specified by the numbers in front of the asterisk; for example if two columns have "2*" and "5*" then the ratio 2:5 will be used when dividing the remaining space.

The following sample code shows how you can add a **Grid** with columns and rows to the window and add a child control to the **Grid**.

```
<Grid>
    <Grid.RowDefinitions>
        <RowDefinition MinHeight="50" MaxHeight="100" />
        <RowDefinition Height="Auto" />
    </Grid.RowDefinitions>
    <Grid.ColumnDefinitions>
        <ColumnDefinition Width="2*" />
        <ColumnDefinition Width="5*" />
    </Grid.ColumnDefinitions>
```

```
    <Label Content="Row 0, Col 0" Grid.Row="0"
        Grid.Column="0" />
</Grid>
```

Additional reading: "MSDN Grid Class"

Canvas

A **Canvas** control can be used if you want to explicitly position child element within the **Canvas**.

The following sample code shows how you can use the Canvas control to explicitly place controls.

```
<Grid>
    <Canvas Height="200" Width="300" Background="Yellow">
        <Canvas Height="100" Width="150" Top="50"
            Left="50" Background="Green">
            <TextBox Width="75" Margin="10"/>
        </Canvas>
    </Canvas>
</Grid>
```

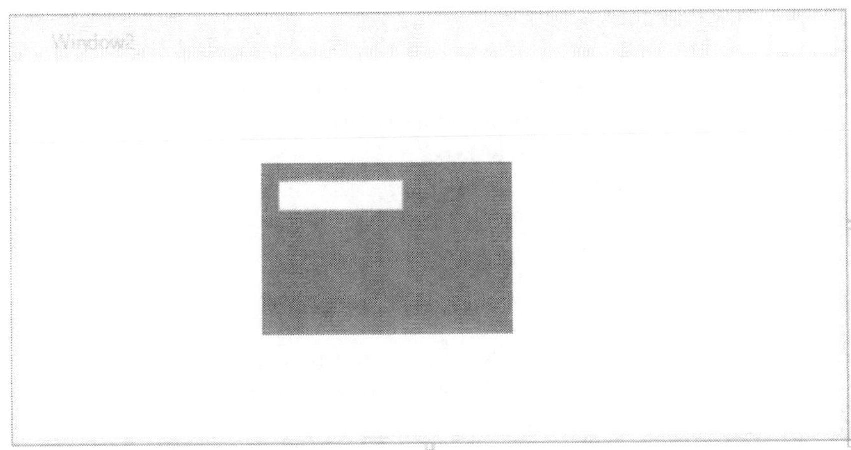

Image 19-4: Canvas

Additional reading: "MSDN Canvas Class"

DockPanel

A **DockPanel** displays its intrinsic controls horizontally or vertically in relative to each other; they dock to the edges of the **DockPanel** control.

The following sample code shows how you can use the **DockPanel** to arrange its intrinsic controls.

```
<Grid>
    <DockPanel LastChildFill="True">
        <Border Height="25" Background="LightBlue"
        BorderBrush="Black" BorderThickness="1"
        DockPanel.Dock="Top">
            <TextBlock Foreground="Black">
                Dock against top border
            </TextBlock>
        </Border>
        <Border Height="25" Background="LightBlue"
        BorderBrush="Black" BorderThickness="1"
        DockPanel.Dock="Top">
            <TextBlock Foreground="Black">
                Dock against top border
            </TextBlock>
        </Border>

        <Border Height="25" Background="LightCoral"
        BorderBrush="Black" BorderThickness="1"
        DockPanel.Dock="Bottom">
            <TextBlock Foreground="Black">
                Dock against bottom border
            </TextBlock>
        </Border>

        <Border Width="200" Background="LightGreen"
        BorderBrush="Black" BorderThickness="1"
        DockPanel.Dock="Left">
            <TextBlock Foreground="Black">
                Dock against left border
            </TextBlock>
        </Border>
```

```
<Border Background="White" BorderBrush="Black"
        BorderThickness="1">
           <TextBlock Foreground="Black">
               The remaining space from the
               control docked against the left
               border
           </TextBlock>
       </Border>
   </DockPanel>
</Grid>
```

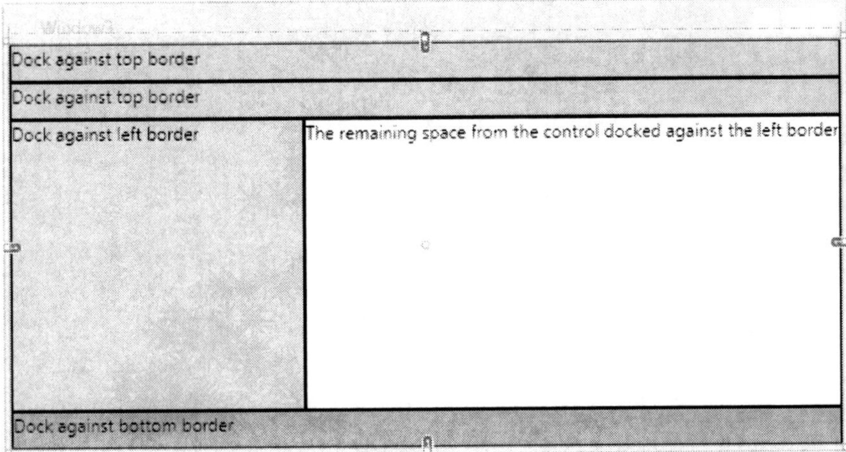

Image 19-5: Dock Panel

Additional reading: "MSDN DockPanel Class"

StackPanel

A **StackPanel** control stacks the intrinsic controls horizontally or vertica-lly in a single line.

The following sample code shows how you can use the **StackPanel** to stack its intrinsic controls.

```
<Grid>
   <StackPanel Width="150" Height="150"
   Orientation="Horizontal" Background="WhiteSmoke">
       <Border Background="LightBlue">
           <TextBlock Foreground="Black" FontSize="12">
               Item #1
           </TextBlock>
       </Border>
       <Border Width="400" Background="LightGreen">
           <TextBlock Foreground="Black" FontSize="14">
               Item #2
           </TextBlock>
       </Border>
       <Border Background="LightPink">
           <TextBlock Foreground="Black" FontSize="16">
               Item #3
           </TextBlock>
       </Border>
       <Border Width="200" Background="LightYellow">
           <TextBlock Foreground="Black" FontSize="18">
               Item #4
           </TextBlock>
       </Border>
       <Border Background="LightGray">
           <TextBlock Foreground="Black" FontSize="20">
               Item #5
           </TextBlock>
       </Border>
   </StackPanel>
</Grid>
```

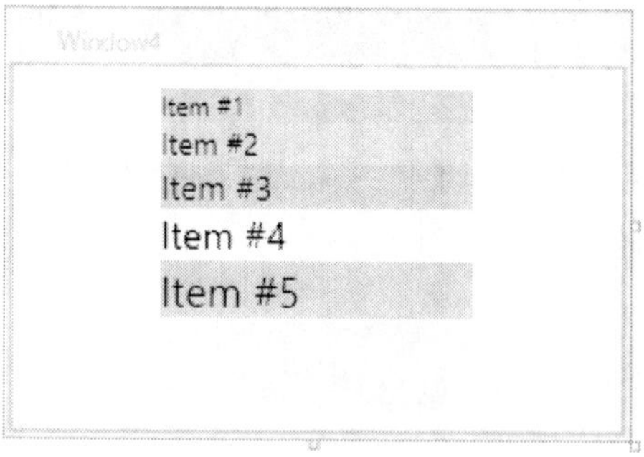

Image 19-6: Stack Panel Vertical

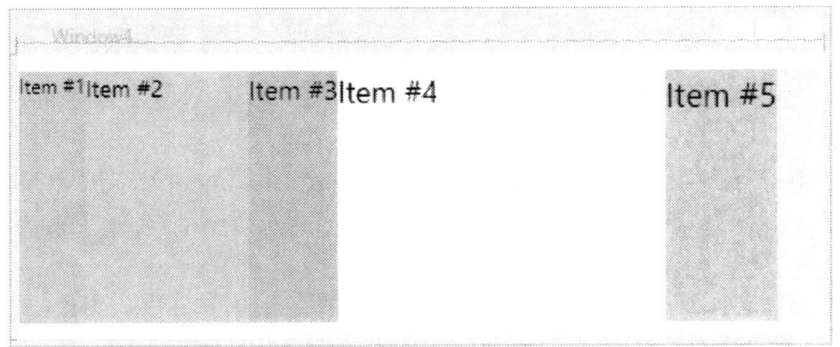

Image 19-7: Stack Panel Horizontal

Additional reading: "MSDN StackPanel Class"

VirtualizingStackPanel

A **VirtualizingStackPanel** works on the same basic principles as a **StackPanel** with the difference that it only creates items for visible items.

The following sample code shows how you can use the **VirtualizingStackPanel** to stack its intrinsic controls.

```
<Grid>
    <VirtualizingStackPanel Width="280" Height="150"
    Background="WhiteSmoke">
        <Border Background="LightBlue">
            <TextBlock Foreground="Black" FontSize="12">
                Item #1</TextBlock>
        </Border>
        <Border Background="LightGreen">
            <TextBlock Foreground="Black" FontSize="14">
                Item #2</TextBlock>
        </Border>
        <Border Background="LightPink">
            <TextBlock Foreground="Black" FontSize="16">
                Item #3</TextBlock>
        </Border>
    </VirtualizingStackPanel>
</Grid>
```

Additional reading: "MSDN VirtualizingStackPanel Class"

WrapPanel

The **WrapPanel** stacks its intrinsic controls from left to right and top to bottom creating a new row when a child control goes over the **WrapPanel** width. You can change the orientation of the intrinsic controls representation inside the **WrapPanel** by setting the **Orientation** attribute.

The following sample code shows how you can use the **WrapPanel** to display controls.

```
<Grid>
    <Border HorizontalAlignment="Left"
    VerticalAlignment="Top" BorderBrush="Black"
    BorderThickness="1" Margin="10">
        <WrapPanel Background="LightGreen" Width="200"
        Height="50">
            <Button Width="200">Button 1</Button>
            <Button>Button 2</Button>
            <Button>Button 3</Button>
        </WrapPanel>
    </Border>
</Grid>
```

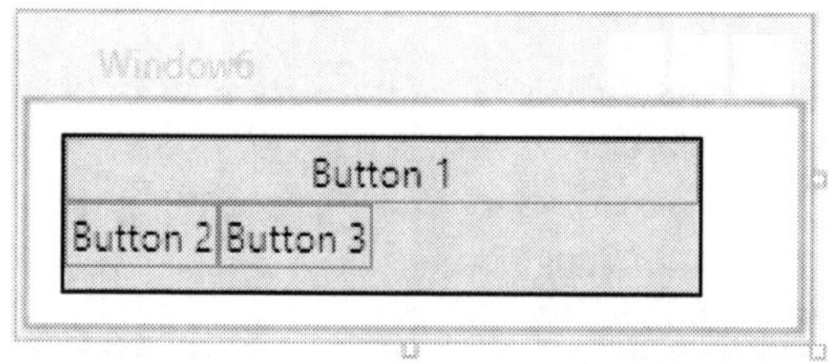

Image 19-8: Wrap Panel

Additional reading: "MSDN WrapPanel Class"

User Control

A **UserControl**, or composite control as it is also called, is a container in which you can place intrinsic controls that together form a unit; for instance, you could create a login control that you then could reuse in other applications.

Creating **UserControls** has several benefits such as being self-contained, easy to maintain, reusable and can be shared across several assemblies.

Just as with the **Window** control the **UserControl** consist of a XAML file and a code behind file and its top-level element is **UserControl**.

Internally in the **UserControl** you can use properties to hold state that you expose to the **Window** that contains the **UserControl**. To make the **Window** control aware that something has happened in the **UserControl,** you can let the **UserControl** publish events that the **Window** control can subscribe to. The **Windows** control can then access the public members of the **UserControl** to use the result.

When adding a **UserControl** to the **Window** control, you have to specify a *namespace prefix* for the **UserControl** in the header of the **Window** control using the following syntax; the assembly name can be omitted if the **UserControl** is in the same assembly as the **Window** control:

xmlns:[your prefix]=***"clr-namespace:***[your namespace],[your assembly name]*"*

Example

The following example shows how you can create a **UserControl** and add it to a **Window** control.

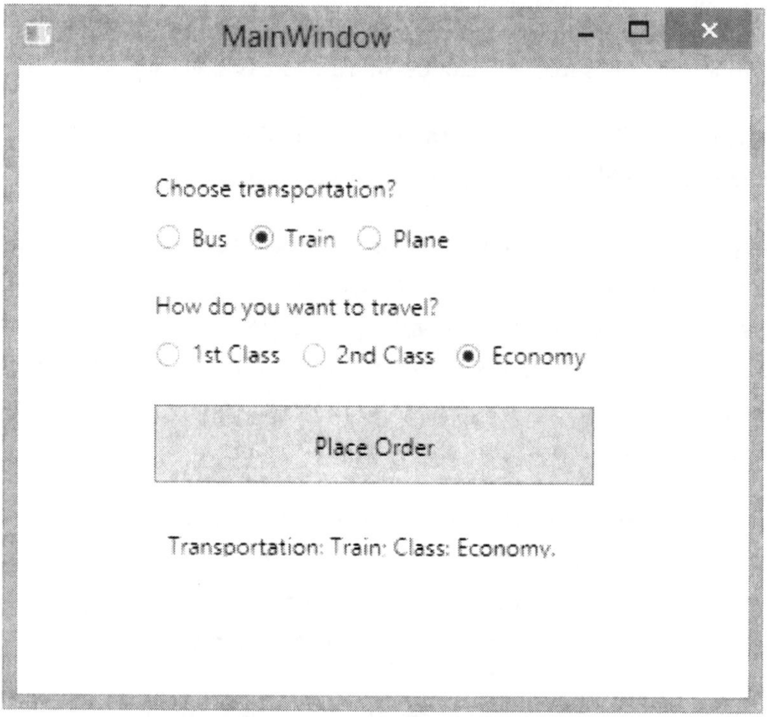

Image 19-9: User Control

The UserControl Designer

To add a **UserControl** to the project, right-click on the project in the Solution Explorer and select **Add-User Control**.

Add the desired intrinsic controls to the **UserControl** design surface and event handlers to the necessary controls; in this sample, we add a **Click** event handler to the button and another to handle the clicks that the radio buttons generate; use the same event handler method for all the radio button controls.

Note that we use two nested **StackPanels** for the two radio button sections; we do this because we want the radio buttons to be displayed horizontally while the radio button group and the corresponding label are displayed vertically.

```
<Grid>
   <Grid.RowDefinitions>
       <RowDefinition Height="1.2*"/>
       <RowDefinition Height="1.2*"/>
       <RowDefinition Height="1*"/>
   </Grid.RowDefinitions>
   <StackPanel Grid.Row="0">
       <Label Content="Choose transportation?"/>
       <StackPanel Grid.Row="0"
       Orientation="Horizontal">
           <RadioButton x:Name="radBus" Content="Bus"
               HorizontalAlignment="Left"
               VerticalAlignment="Top" Margin="5"
               GroupName="Transport"
               Checked="radio_Checked"
               IsChecked="True"/>
           <RadioButton x:Name="radTrain"
               Content="Train"
               HorizontalAlignment="Left"
               VerticalAlignment="Top" Margin="5"
               GroupName="Transport"
               Checked="radio_Checked"/>
           <RadioButton x:Name="radPlane"
               Content="Plane"
               HorizontalAlignment="Left"
               VerticalAlignment="Top" Margin="5"
               GroupName="Transport"
               Checked="radio_Checked"/>
       </StackPanel>
   </StackPanel>

   <StackPanel Grid.Row="1">
       <Label Content="How do you want to travel?"/>
       <StackPanel Grid.Row="1"
           Orientation="Horizontal">
           <RadioButton x:Name="rad1Class"
               Content="1st Class"
               HorizontalAlignment="Left"
               VerticalAlignment="Top" Margin="5"
               GroupName="Class" Checked="radio_Checked"
               IsChecked="True"/>
```

```
            <RadioButton x:Name="rad2Class"
                Content="2nd Class"
                HorizontalAlignment="Left"
                VerticalAlignment="Top" Margin="5"
                GroupName="Class"
                Checked="radio_Checked"/>
            <RadioButton x:Name="radEconomy"
                Content="Economy"
                HorizontalAlignment="Left"
                VerticalAlignment="Top" Margin="5"
                GroupName="Class"
                Checked="radio_Checked"/>
        </StackPanel>
    </StackPanel>

    <Button x:Name="btnOrder" Content="Place Order"
        Margin="5,5,5,5" Grid.Row="3"
        Click="btnOrder_Click"/>
</Grid>
```

The UserControl Code Behind

When the intrinsic controls have been added to the **UserControl,** we switch to the code behind (.cs) file and write the logic of the control.

We need to be able to hold state for which radio button has been selected in the two radio button groups; we do this by adding two properties called **Transportation** and **TravelClass** with public getters and private setters. We also want to give the developer who is using this **UserControl** to fetch a formatted string with the selected order information; to achieve this we add a third property, **Order**, with only a getter that returns the formatted string containing the values that the user has selected.

We also want the Window control to be able to subscribe to an event called **OrderPlaced** that is triggered when the user clicks the **Order** button; to achieve this we have to add an **EventHandler** with that name that is triggered from the **Order** buttons' click event called *btnOrder_Click*. Remember to check that the event is not null before raising the event.

The last thing we need to add to the **UserControl** is the radio button event handler, *radio_Checked*, which all the radio buttons will call when one of the radio buttons is clicked. In this event handler method, we will first write a switch that checks the **GroupName** property of the clicked radio button, then we will assign a value to the appropriate property; the value is simply the content displayed in the selected radio button.

```
namespace XAML_Controls
{
    public partial class TravelControl : UserControl
    {
        public event EventHandler<EventArgs> OrderPlaced;

        public string Transportation
            { get; private set; }
        public string TravelClass { get; private set; }
        public string Order {
            get
            {
                return String.Format(
                "Transportation: {0}; Class: {1}.",
                Transportation, TravelClass);
            }
        }

        public TravelControl()
        {
            InitializeComponent();
        }

        private void radio_Checked(object sender,
        RoutedEventArgs e)
        {
            switch (((RadioButton)e.Source).GroupName)
            {
                case "Transport":
                    Transportation =
                        ((RadioButton)e.Source)
                            .Content.ToString();
                    break;
```

```
                case "Class":
                    TravelClass =
                        ((RadioButton)e.Source)
                            .Content.ToString();
                    break;
            }
        }

        private void btnOrder_Click(object sender,
        RoutedEventArgs e)
        {
            if (OrderPlaced != null)
                OrderPlaced(this, EventArgs.Empty);
        }
    }
}
```

The Window Designer

When the **UserControl** is finished, we add it to the **Window** designer along with a **Label** control, *lblResult*, which will display the message that will be displayed from the **UserControl** event handler method. Do not forget that you need to specify the namespace prefix in the **Window** header.

When adding the **UserControl** event handler method, name it *travelSelector_OrderPlaced*; this is the name that will be used in the code behind to implement the event handler method.

```
<Window x:Class="XAML_Controls.MainWindow"
    xmlns="http://schemas.microsoft.com/winfx/2006/
        xaml/presentation"
    xmlns:x="http://schemas.microsoft.com/winfx/
        2006/xaml"
    Title="MainWindow" Height="353" Width="835"
    xmlns:travel="clr-namespace:XAML_Controls">

    <Grid>
        <travel:TravelControl x:Name="travelSelector"
            OrderPlaced="travelSelector_OrderPlaced"
            Margin="556,10,10,138" />
```

```
        <Label x:Name="lblResult" Content="Order result"
            Margin="563,189,14,101"  />
    </Grid>
</Window>
```

The Window Code Behind

In the **Window** code behind (.cs) file, we assign the **Order** property value of the **UserControl** to the label.

```
private void travelSelector_OrderPlaced(object sender,
EventArgs e)
{
    lblResult.Content = travelSelector.Order;
}
```

Data Binding

Almost all UI applications connect to a data source such as files, databases or web services to retrieve and store data.

Data binding connect UI control and data source in a way that if one changes, both reflect the change.

There are three components related to data binding: ***Binding Source:*** This is your data source which typically is a property on an object; for instance the FirstName property of a Student object. ***Binding Target:*** This is a dependency property on one of your XAML elements; it could bind the Context property of a TextBox control. ***Binding Object:*** This is an object that connect source and target; it can contain a converter if the data types differ.

Dependency properties wrap around regular properties and register with the run-time to notify interested parties when data changes are made.

Additional reading: "Dependency Properties Overview"

You can also specify the directionality of the data by assigning a value to the **Mode** property of the **Binding** object.

Mode	Description
TwoWay	Updates the source or the target when one of them changes.
OneWay	Updates the target when the source changes.
OneTime	Updates the target when the application starts or the **DataContext** property of the target is changed.
OneWayTo-Source	Updates the source when the target property changes.
Default	Uses the default **Mode** setting of the target property.

In the following sample code, the ***Binding Source*** is the FirstName property of the Student object, the ***Binding Target*** is the Text property of the TextBlock element and the ***Binding Object*** is defined within the braces.

```
<Grid>
   <TextBlock Text="{Binding
       Source={StaticResource student},
       Path=FirstName, Mode=TwoWay}"/>
</Grid>
```

Additional reading: "Data Binding Overview"

Connecting to a Static Resource

Static resources can be used if you know that the data won't change; you specify the data directly in the XAML inside a **Windows.Resources** element.

You also must create a namespace prefix in the **Window** header that specifies the namespace and assembly where the class you want to use is located.

Each instance of the class you use must have a unique key defined; you define the key by using the **x:Key** attribute of the resource element.

The following sample code shows how you can implement a static resource and use it in the UI.

The Class Used In The Static Resource

```
namespace XAML_Controls
{
    class StaticStudent
    {
        public string FirstName { get; set; }
        public string LastName { get; set; }
        public DateTime DOB { get; set; }
    }
}
```

The Static Resource XAML

Note that the namespace specified in the prefix is the namespace of the class. Also note that the Window.Resources element is above the Grid element.

```
<Window x:Class="XAML_Controls.StaticResource"
    xmlns="http://schemas.microsoft.com/winfx/2006/
        xaml/presentation"
    xmlns:x="http://schemas.microsoft.com/winfx/2006/
        xaml"
    xmlns:loc="clr-namespace:XAML_Controls"
    Title="StaticResource" Height="300" Width="300">
    <Window.Resources>
        <loc:StaticStudent x:Key="student1"
            FirstName="Jonas"
            LastName="Fagerberg"
            DOB="1970-05-04"/>
    </Window.Resources>
<Grid></Grid>
```

Using The Static Resource

Note that the *Binding Source* of the StackPanel is declared within a **StackPanel.DataContext** element. Also note that the Binding keyword is used with the Path attribute to connect the object property with the Text property of the TextBlock controls.

```
<Grid>
    <StackPanel>
        <StackPanel.DataContext>
            <Binding Source=
                "{StaticResource student1}" />
        </StackPanel.DataContext>

        <TextBlock Text="{Binding Path=FirstName}" />
        <TextBlock Text="{Binding Path=LastName}" />
        <TextBlock Text="{Binding Path=DOB}" />
    </StackPanel>
</Grid>
```

Data Binding Using C# Code

You can create data binding using C# code in the code behind.

The XAML code

```
<Grid>
    <StackPanel Orientation="Horizontal">
        <TextBlock Name="FirstName" Margin="5"/>
        <TextBlock Name="LastName" Margin="5"/>
        <TextBlock Name="DOB" Margin="5"/>
    </StackPanel>
</Grid>
```

The C# code

Create an instance of the **StaticStudent** class and assign values to its properties. Then create an instance of the Binding class and set the Source property to the **StaticStudent** instance and set the Path property to a PropertyPath instance holding the name of the **StaticStudent** instance property name that you want to bind to. Lastly, bind the Text property of the TextBlock control to the binding object you created.

```
void SetUpDataBinding()
{
    StaticStudent student = new StaticStudent();
    student.FirstName = "Jonas";
    student.LastName = "Fagerberg";
    student.DOB = new DateTime(1970, 5, 4);

    Binding fistNameBinding = new Binding();
    fistNameBinding.Source = student;
    fistNameBinding.Path = new PropertyPath("FirstName");
    Binding lastNameBinding = new Binding();
    lastNameBinding.Source = student;
    lastNameBinding.Path = new PropertyPath("LastName");
    Binding dobBinding = new Binding();
    dobBinding.Source = student;
    dobBinding.Path = new PropertyPath("DOB");

    FirstName.SetBinding(TextBlock.TextProperty,
        fistNameBinding);
    LastName.SetBinding(TextBlock.TextProperty,
        lastNameBinding);

    DOB.SetBinding(TextBlock.TextProperty, dobBinding);
}
```

Connecting to a Collection

WPF includes several controls that can bind to a collection and they all inherit from the **ItemsControl** class, such as **ListBox**, **ListView**, **ComboBox** and **TreeView**.

You bind the collection to the control using the **ItemsSource** property.

If you want the list control to be automatically updated when new items are added or removed from the collection then the collection must implement the **InotifyPropertyChanged** interface that raises a **PropertyChanged** event when a change has been made.

Additional Reading: "INotifyPropertyChanged Interface"

The following sample shows how you can implement the **Inotify-PropertyChanged** interface in the object class that is added to a **BindingList** list which is used as an **ItemSource** for a **ListView** control in the **Window**.

The DemoStudent Class (implements INotifyPropertyChanged)

```
class DemoStudent : INotifyPropertyChanged
{
    public event PropertyChangedEventHandler
        PropertyChanged;
    private string fName = String.Empty;
    private string lName = String.Empty;

    public Guid Id { get; private set; }
    public string FirstName {
        get { return fName; }
        set {
            if (value != this.fName)
            {
                this.fName = value;
                NotifyPropertyChanged();
            }
        }
    }

    public string LastName {
        get { return lName; }
        set {
            if (value != this.lName)
            {
                this.lName = value;
                NotifyPropertyChanged();
            }
        }
    }
```

```
    public DemoStudent(string firstName, string lastName)
    {
        Id = Guid.NewGuid();
        FirstName = firstName;
        LastName = lastName;
    }

    // This method will be called when a property
    // value is set.
    private void NotifyPropertyChanged(
    [CallerMemberName] String propertyName = "")
    {
        if (PropertyChanged != null)
        {
            PropertyChanged(this, new
                PropertyChangedEventArgs(propertyName));
        }
    }
}
```

The XAML Code

```
<Grid>
    <StackPanel>
        <ListView Name="StudentListView" Height="100"/>

        <Button Name="ChangeValue"
            Content="Change value" Height="30"
            Click="ChangeValue_Click"/>
    </StackPanel>
</Grid>
```

The Code Behind C# Code

When the user clicks the button, the first name in the list changes and the change is reflected in the **ListView** control.

```
public partial class ConnectToCollection : Window
{
    BindingList<DemoStudent> studentList =
        new BindingList<DemoStudent>();
```

```
    public ConnectToCollection()
    {
        InitializeComponent();
        SetUpCollection();
    }



    void SetUpCollection()
    {
        studentList.Add(new DemoStudent(
            "Name 1", "Last name 1"));
        studentList.Add(new DemoStudent(
            "Name 2", "Last name 2"));
        studentList.Add(new DemoStudent(
            "Name 3", "Last name 3"));

        StudentListView.ItemsSource = studentList;
        StudentListView.DisplayMemberPath = "FirstName";
    }

    private void ChangeValue_Click(object sender,
    RoutedEventArgs e)
    {
        var student = (
            from s in studentList
            select s).First();

        student.FirstName = "Jonas";
    }
}
```

Additional reading: "ObservableCollection<T> Class"

Connecting to a Database

You can connect a database to a WPF ListView control by using an entity from an Entity Data Model (EDM). Set the **ItemSource** property to the entity converted to a list using the **ToList** method and the **Display-MemeberPath** to the column you want to display in the list.

You could implement a combination of an EDM and a collection containing objects of a class implementing the **INotifyPropertyChanged** interface to achieve immediate UI updates.

This smple code shows a simple data binding between a ListView and an EDM.

The XAML Code

```
<Grid>
    <StackPanel>
        <ListView Name="StudentListView" Height="100"/>
        <Button Name="ChangeValue"
            Content="Change value" Height="30"
            Click="ChangeValue_Click"/>
    </StackPanel>
</Grid>
```

The Code Behind C# Code

```
public partial class ConnectToEDM : Window
{
    SchoolDBEntities se = new SchoolDBEntities();

    public ConnectToEDM()
    {
        InitializeComponent();
        SetUpEDM();
    }

    void SetUpEDM()
    {
        StudentListView.ItemsSource =
            se.Students.ToList();
        StudentListView.DisplayMemberPath = "FirstName";
    }
```

```
    private void ChangeValue_Click(object sender,
    RoutedEventArgs e)
    {
        var student = (from s in se.Students
            select s).First();

        student.FirstName = "Jonas";
        se.SaveChanges();
        // Will update the ListView items
        StudentListView.ItemsSource =
            se.Students.ToList();
    }
}
```

Data Templates

With data templates you can specify what data will be displayed in each item in the list. To create a template, add a ***Control*.ItemTemplate** element inside the control element. Inside the **ItemTemplate** element, you then add a **DataTemplate** element in which you place the item controls.

The following sample code shows how you can create a template that displays the first and last name on the same row with formatted text.

Template sample for a ListView

```
<Grid>
    <StackPanel>
        <ListView Name="StudentListViewWithTemplate"
            Height="100">
            <ListView.ItemTemplate>
                <DataTemplate>
                    <StackPanel Orientation="Horizontal">
                        <TextBlock Text="{Binding
                        Path=FirstName}" Margin="0,0,5,0"
                        FontSize="22" Background="Black"
                        Foreground="White" />
                        <TextBlock FontSize="22"
                        Text="{Binding Path=LastName}"/>
                    </StackPanel>
                </DataTemplate>
```

```
            </ListView.ItemTemplate>
        </ListView>

        <Button Name="ChangeValue"
            Content="Change value" Height="30"
            Click="ChangeValue_Click"/>
    </StackPanel>
</Grid>
```

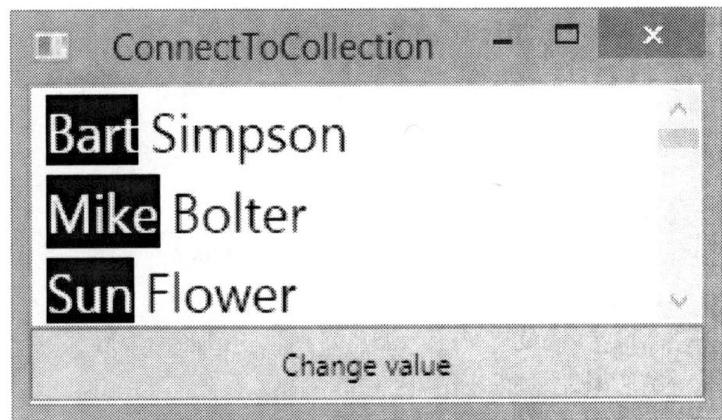

Image 19-11: List View Template

Additional Reading: "MSDN Data Templating Overview"

UI Styling

Styling is a way to make your UI look more appealing to the user. You can format every control individually, but that would be very time-consuming and difficult to maintain; with XAML, you can create reusable styles that can be used with multiple controls.

There are different elements that have certain uses when it comes to styling, such as templates, styles and brushes. These elements are reusable, which means that if the look of the controls using that particular element needs to change, the change only has to be made in one place. It also saves space and makes the XAML more readable.

All WPF controls have a **Resources** property, which means that if you set a resource on a root element, it will change all child elements. If you want global resources for the entire application, you can add the resource to the **App.xaml** file.

When declaring a resource, you need to give it a unique key value because it is stored in a **ResourceDictionary**. You reference the resource using the **Key** name *{**StaticResource** [resource key]}*.

This sample code shows how you can define a **LinearGradientBrush** resource at the **Window** root level and a brush at **Application** level applying the resources to a **Label** control.

App.xaml

```
<Application x:Class="XAML_Controls.App"
    xmlns="http://schemas.microsoft.com/winfx/2006/
        xaml/presentation"
    xmlns:x=http://schemas.microsoft.com/winfx/2006/xaml
    StartupUri="MainWindow.xaml">
    <Application.Resources>
        <SolidColorBrush x:Key="MyBrush" Color="Yellow" />
    </Application.Resources>
</Application>
```

The Window

```
<Window x:Class="XAML_Controls.MainWindow"
    xmlns="http://schemas.microsoft.com/winfx/2006/
        xaml/presentation"
    xmlns:x="http://schemas.microsoft.com/winfx/
        2006/xaml"
    Title="MainWindow" Height="353" Width="835"
    xmlns:travel="clr-namespace:XAML_Controls">
    <Window.Resources>
        <LinearGradientBrush x:Key="Gradient"
        StartPoint="0.5, 0.5" EndPoint="1.5, 1.5" >
            <GradientStop Color="LightBlue" Offset="0" />
            <GradientStop Color="Blue" Offset="0.75" />
        </LinearGradientBrush>
    </Window.Resources>
```

```
<Grid>
   <Label x:Name="lblResult" Content="Order result"
       Margin="563,189,14,101"
       Background="{StaticResource Gradient}"
       Foreground="{StaticResource MyBrush}"/>
</Grid>
```

Image 19-12: UI Styling

Styles

A style can be used to define settings for a control type such as **Text-Block** making it possible to target the desired controls of the specified type and set default property values for them. You must assign the style to the controls that you want to style using the **Style** property.

```
<Window x:Class="XAML_Controls.MainWindow"
   xmlns="http://schemas.microsoft.com/winfx/2006/
       xaml/presentation"
   xmlns:x="http://schemas.microsoft.com/winfx/
       2006/xaml"
   Title="MainWindow" Height="353" Width="835"
   xmlns:travel="clr-namespace:XAML_Controls">
   <Window.Resources>
       <Style TargetType="TextBlock"
       x:Key="BlockStyle1">
           <Setter Property="FontSize" Value="20" />
           <Setter Property="Background"
               Value="WhiteSmoke" />
           <Setter Property="Foreground">
               <Setter.Value>
                   <LinearGradientBrush
                       StartPoint="0.5,0"
                       EndPoint="0.5,1">
```

```
                    <LinearGradientBrush.GradientStops>
                        <GradientStop Offset="0.0"
                            Color="LightGreen" />
                        <GradientStop Offset="1.0"
                            Color="DarkGreen" />

                    </LinearGradientBrush.GradientStops>
                    </LinearGradientBrush>
                </Setter.Value>
            </Setter>
        </Style>
    </Window.Resources>

    <Grid>
        <TextBlock Name="TextBlock1"
            Style="{StaticResource BlockStyle1}"
            Margin="22,41,0,0"
            Text="TextBlock" Width="120"/>
    </Grid>
```

TextBlock

Image 19-13: Text Block

Additional reading: "styling and templating wpf"

Property Triggers

A property trigger can be used to trigger on a property value for instance if you hover over a control with the mouse.

The following sample code shows how you can trigger on the **IsMouseOver** property and change the style of a button when the mouse is hovering over one of them.

```
<Window x:Class="XAML_Controls.MainWindow"
    xmlns="http://schemas.microsoft.com/winfx/2006/
        xaml/presentation"
    xmlns:x="http://schemas.microsoft.com/winfx/
        2006/xaml"
    Title="MainWindow" Height="353" Width="835"
    xmlns:travel="clr-namespace:XAML_Controls">
    <Window.Resources>
        <Style TargetType="Button">
            <Style.Triggers>
                <Trigger Property="IsMouseOver"
                Value="True">
                    <Setter Property="FontWeight"
                    Value="Bold" />
                </Trigger>
            </Style.Triggers>
        </Style>
    </Window.Resources>
```

The button text The button text

Image 19-14: Property Trigger for Button

Dynamic Transformations and Animations

Animations are sometimes used when transitioning between states; you need three things to create a transition: An animation, the most common of which is **DoubleAnimation** element. Second, you need a storyboard to wrap the animation in, so use the **Storyboard** elements' **TargetName** and **TargetProperty**. Third, you need a trigger to wrap your storyboard in, use a **BeginStoryboard** element in the **EventTrigger** element.

Additional reading: "msdn wpf Animation Overview"

This sample code shows how you can create a transformation on an image making it larger and rotating 180 degrees when clicking it.

```
<Window.Resources>
   <Style TargetType="Image" x:Key="ImageStyle">
       <Setter Property="Height" Value="25"/>
       <Setter Property="RenderTransformOrigin"
           Value="0.5,0.5"/>
       <Setter Property="RenderTransform">
           <Setter.Value>
               <RotateTransform Angle="0"/>
           </Setter.Value>
       </Setter>
       <Style.Triggers>
           <EventTrigger RoutedEvent="Image.MouseDown">
               <BeginStoryboard>
                   <Storyboard>
                       <DoubleAnimation Storyboard
                           .TargetProperty="Height"
                           From="25" To="40"
                           Duration="0:0:1"/>
                       <DoubleAnimation Storyboard
                           .TargetProperty=
                           "RenderTransform.Angle"
                           From="0" To="180"
                           Duration="0:0:1"/>
                   </Storyboard>
               </BeginStoryboard>
           </EventTrigger>
       </Style.Triggers>
   </Style>
</Window.Resources>

<Grid>
   <Image HorizontalAlignment="Left"
       Margin="24,20,0,0" VerticalAlignment="Top"
       Style="{StaticResource ImageStyle}"
       Source="C:/Sample Files/info.png" Height="25" />
</Grid>
```

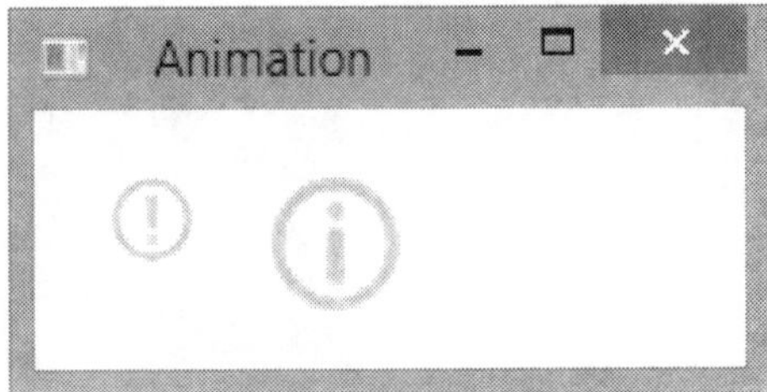

Image 19-15: Image Animation

Application Performance

To enhance the experience for users, you should take advantage of distributing the work to multiple threads simultaneously. We will see how the *Task Parallel Library* will solve this and how we can perform long-running tasks without blocking threads as well as how to access resources concurrently from multiple threads.

You should avoid executing long-running tasks on the UI thread because that will render the UI unresponsive. Most of the processors today have multiple cores; be sure to utilize that by using multiple threads in the application to improve performance.

Tasks

The **Task** class will enable you to perform multiple tasks in parallel on different threads. The *Task Parallel Library* handles the thread pool in the background to assign tasks to threads; with this library you can chain and pause tasks, wait for tasks to complete and perform other operations.

You create a task by using an instance of the **Task** class passing in an **Action** delegate that points to the method to be executed; this *static* method must be implemented and cannot return a value. If you need to return a value, you can use the **Func** class or a **Task<TResult>** instead.

Using an Action Delegate to Create a Task

```
Task taskWithMethod = new Task(new Action(Pause));

private void TaskWithMethod_Click(object sender,
RoutedEventArgs e)
{
   taskWithMethod.Start();
}

private static void Pause()
{
   Thread.Sleep(3000);
   MessageBox.Show("Finished: " +
       DateTime.Now.ToLongTimeString());
}
```

Using an Anonymous Delegate to Create a Task

If you want to execute a method that has a single purpose you can implement it using an anonymous delegate.

```
Task taskWithDelegate = new Task(delegate
{
   Thread.Sleep(3000);
   MessageBox.Show("Finished: " +
       DateTime.Now.ToLongTimeString());
});

private void TaskWithDelegate_Click(object sender,
RoutedEventArgs e)
{
   taskWithDelegate.Start();
}
```

Creating Tasks Using Lambda Expressions

Lambda is a shorthand way to define anonymous delegates that can take parameters and return a value; Lambda expressions follow the form (input parameters) => expression; the Lambda operator (=>) reads as "Goes to". You can pass in variables to the expression in the parenthesis on the left side of the operator; for instance the expression

(x, y) => x > y would return **true** if **x** is greater than **y**, otherwise it would return **false**.

A Lambda expression can be used with a simple expression, target an implemented method or an anonymous method defined by a code block within curly braces on the form *(input parameters) => { C# code }*.

Using Lambda expressions is the recommended way to implement **Tasks** because it is a concise way of declaring delegates that have a tendency to become complex.

Using a Lambda Expression and an Implemented Function to Create a Task

```
// Equivalent to:
// Task task1 = new Task( delegate(Pause) );
Task taskWithLambda = new Task(() => Pause());

private void TaskWithLambda_Click(object sender,
RoutedEventArgs e)
{
    taskWithLambda.Start();
}

private static void Pause()
{
    Thread.Sleep(3000);
    MessageBox.Show("Finished: " +
        DateTime.Now.ToLongTimeString());
}
```

Using a Lambda Expression and an Anonymous Delegate to Create a Task

```
Task taskWithLambdaAnonymous = new Task(() =>
{
    Thread.Sleep(3000);
    MessageBox.Show("Finished: " +
        DateTime.Now.ToLongTimeString());
});
```

```
private void TaskWithLambdaAnonymous_Click(
object sender, RoutedEventArgs e)
{
    taskWithLambdaAnonymous.Start();
}
```

Additional reading: "Lambda Expressions (C# Programming Guide)"

Controlling Task Execution

You can use three different methods to start queuing a **Task** for execution; the **Task.Factory.StartNew** method is highly configurable using its parameters.

Three Ways to start a Task

```
Task task1 = new Task(() => Console.WriteLine(
    "Task 1 has completed."));
task1.Start();

var task2 = Task.Factory.StartNew(() =>
    Console.WriteLine("Task 2 has completed."));

// A shorter way of calling the
// Task.Factory.StartNew method
var task3 = Task.Run(() => Console.WriteLine(
    "Task 3 has completed. "));
```

Waiting on Tasks

Sometimes you need to wait on the execution of a **Task**; this can be if you need to use a result of the **Task** or if you need to handle exceptions that might be thrown by the **Task**.

There are three methods that you can use to wait on a **Task**; the **Task.Wait** method waits on a specific Task; the **Task.WaitAll** will wait on multiple **Tasks** to finish, and the **Task.WaitAny** will wait until any one **Task** in a collection of tasks has finished.

The following methods and variable will be used in the upcoming code samples.

```
private static string result = String.Empty;

private static void LongRunningTaskA() {
    Thread.Sleep(3000); result = "LongRunningTaskA"; }

private static void LongRunningTaskB() {
    Thread.Sleep(1000); result = "LongRunningTaskB"; }

private static void LongRunningTaskC() {
    Thread.Sleep(3000); result = "LongRunningTaskC"; }
```

Wait On One Task

The execution will wait until the **Task** has completed; the Label content will display *LongRunningTaskA* when the task has completed.

```
private void WaitOnOneTask_Click(object sender,
RoutedEventArgs e)
{
    var taskA = Task.Run(() => LongRunningTaskA());
    taskA.Wait();
    lblTest.Content = result;
}
```

Wait On Any Task

The execution will wait until one of the tasks in the **Task** list has completed; the Label content will display *LongRunningTaskB* when the task has completed because that **Task** finishes first.

```
private void WaitOnAnyTask_Click(object sender,
RoutedEventArgs e)
{
    Task[] tasks = new Task[3]
    {
        Task.Run( () => LongRunningTaskA()),
        Task.Run( () => LongRunningTaskB()),
        Task.Run( () => LongRunningTaskC())
    };
```

```
    // Wait for any of the tasks to complete
    Task.WaitAny(tasks);
    lblTest.Content = result;
}
```

Wait On All Tasks

The execution will wait until all of the tasks in the **Task** list have completed; the Label content will display *LongRunningTaskC* when tasks have completed because that **Task** finishes last.

```
Private void WaitOnAnyTask_Click(object sender,
RoutedEventArgs e)
{
    Task[] tasks = new Task[3]
    {
        Task.Run( () => LongRunningTaskA()),
        Task.Run( () => LongRunningTaskB()),
        Task.Run( () => LongRunningTaskC())
    };

    // Wait for all of the tasks to complete
    Task.WaitAll(tasks);
    lblTest.Content = result;
}
```

Return a Value from a Task

To return a value from **Task,** you need to use the generic **Task<TResult>** class; when the **Task<TResult>** has finished its execution, the return value will reside in a property named **Result** in the **Task<TResult>** instance that you declared.

Example

When the Task finishes its execution, a **StaticStudent** instance is returned in the **Return** property.

```
private void ReturnAValueFromATask_Click(object sender,
RoutedEventArgs e)
{
    Task<StaticStudent> task1 =
        Task.Run<StaticStudent>(() => new StaticStudent()
            { FirstName="Jonas", LastName="Fagerberg" });

    lblTest.Content = String.Format("{0} {1}",
        task1.Result.FirstName,
        task1.Result.LastName);
}
```

Cancel a Task

During certain circumstances, you might want to give the user the possibility to cancel a long-running **Task**; it would however be dangerous to just end the **Task,** so the *Task Parallel Library* uses cancellation tokens to support cooperative cancellations.

To be able to cancel a **Task,** you need to create a cancellation token when creating the **Task**. You then pass that token to the delegate method. You cancel the **Task** by calling the **Cancel** method on the **CancellationTokenSource** instance that created the token instance. In the method where the **Task** was created, you can check the status of cancellation token.

Cancel a Task without Throwing an Exception

First, we create a variable to hold the **Task**, a **CancellationTokenSource** instance to create the cancellation token and a **CancellationToken** variable to hold the token. In the first **Click** event, method, we assign a newly created token to the **CancellationToken** variable, then we start the **Task**. In the second **Click** event method, we cancel the **Task**. The **DoWork** method is executed in the **Task**; note that we check if cancellation has been requested.

```
Task task;
CancellationTokenSource cts = new
CancellationTokenSource();
```

```
CancellationToken ct;
private void CancelATask_Click(object sender,
RoutedEventArgs e)
{
    result = String.Empty;
    ct = cts.Token;
    task = Task.Run(() => doWork(ct));
}

private void CancelTheTask_Click(object sender,
RoutedEventArgs e)
{
    cts.Cancel();
    lblTest.Content = result;
}

private void doWork(CancellationToken token)
{
    for (int i = 0; i < 3; i++)
    {
        // Check for cancellation.
        if (token.IsCancellationRequested)
        {
            result = "Cancelled";
            return;
        }

        Thread.Sleep(1000);

        // Continue if the task has not been
        // cancelled
        result = "Finished";
    }
}
```

Cancel a Task Throwing an Exception

If you want the **Task** to throw an exception if canceled, then you need to call the **ThrowIfCancellationRequested** method on the token instance; an **OperationCanceledException** exception will be thrown if the **Task** is canceled.

```
Task task;
CancellationTokenSource cts = new
CancellationTokenSource();
CancellationToken ct;

private void CancelATaskThrow_Click(object sender,
RoutedEventArgs e)
{
    result = String.Empty;
    ct = cts.Token;
    task = Task.Run(() => doWorkThrow(ct1));
}

private void CancelTheTaskThrow_Click(object sender,
RoutedEventArgs e)
{
    try
    {
        cts.Cancel();
        if (ct.IsCancellationRequested)
            throw new OperationCanceledException(ct);
    }
    catch (OperationCanceledException ex)
    {
        lblTest.Content = "Cancelled";
    }
}

private void doWorkThrow(CancellationToken token)
{
    token.ThrowIfCancellationRequested();
    Thread.Sleep(5000);
}
```

Additional reading: "How to: Cancel a Task and Its Children" and "Task Cancellation C#"

Parallel Tasks

The **Parallel** class in the *Task Parallel Library* contains a number of methods that can be used if you want to execute several tasks simultaneously.

A Fixed Set of Tasks

If you have a fixed set of **Tasks** that you want to execute simultaneously, you can use the **Parallel.Invoke** method.

The result after executing this **Task** list would be *MethodC MethodB MethodA* because that's the order the methods finish.

```
Private static void MethodA() { Thread.Sleep(3000);
   result += "MethodA "; }
private static void MethodB() { Thread.Sleep(2000);
   result += "MethodB "; }
private static void MethodC() { Thread.Sleep(1000);
   result += "MethodC "; }

private void ExecuteFixedSetOfTasks_Click(
object sender, RoutedEventArgs e)
{
   result = String.Empty;

   Parallel.Invoke(
       () => MethodA(),
       () => MethodB(),
       () => MethodC()
   );

   lblTest.Content = result;
}
```

Parallel Iterations

If you have a need to run loops in parallel, you can do so using the **Parallel.For** or **Parallel.Foreach** methods; both have many overloads for different scenarios.

Parallel For

The *from* and *to* parameters of the loop are of the type **Int32** and the *index* parameter is executed as an **Action<Int32>** once per iteration.

```
private void ParallelLoops_Click(object sender,
RoutedEventArgs e)
{
    double[] array = ParallelFor();
}

private double[] ParallelFor()
{
    int from = 0;
    int to = 500000;
    double[] array = new double[to];
    Parallel.For(from, to, index =>
    {
        array[index] = Math.Sqrt(index);
    });

    return array;
}
```

Parallel Foreach

The simplest version of this overloaded method takes two parameters one collection of type **IEnumerable<TSource>** that you want to iterate over and one **Action<TSource>** that is the delegate function that will be executed once per iteration.

```
private void ParallelLoops_Click(object sender,
RoutedEventArgs e)
{
    var students = new List<StaticStudent>();
    students.Add(new StaticStudent());
    Parallel.ForEach(students, student =>
        ParallelForeach(student));
}
```

```
private void ParallelForeach(StaticStudent student)
{
    student.FirstName = "Demo Name";
    student.LastName = "Demo Last name";
}
```

Additional reading: "MSDN Data Parallelism (Task Parallel Library)"

Parallel LINQ

Language-Integrated Query (LINQ) supports parallel execution through an implementation called *Parallel LINQ (PLINQ)*. You can use *PLINQ* when iterating over **IEnumerable** collections by calling the **AsParallel** method

Additional reading: "MSDN Parallel LINQ (PLINQ)"

```
private void ParallelLoops_Click(object sender,
RoutedEventArgs e)
{
    // Parallel LINQ (PLINQ)
    var SelectedStudents =
        from student in students.AsParallel()
        where student.LastName == "Smith"
        select student;
}
```

Handling Task Exceptions

When exceptions are thrown from tasks, the *Task Parallel Library* will bundle any exceptions from joined tasks into an **AggregateException** object where all exceptions that has been thrown is stored in the **InnerExceptions** collection property.

You can handle exceptions by waiting until the Task has finished; this is done by calling the **Task.Wait** method in a **try** block and implementing a catch that will catch the **AggregateException**.

```
private void HandleException_Click(object sender,
RoutedEventArgs e)
{
    CancellationTokenSource cts =
        new CancellationTokenSource();
    CancellationToken ct;
    ct = cts.Token;
    var task = Task.Run(() => doWorkThrow(ct), ct);
    cts.Cancel();

    try
    {
        task.Wait();
    }
    catch (AggregateException ae)
    {
        foreach (var inner in ae.InnerExceptions)
        {
            if (inner is TaskCanceledException)
            {
                lblTest.Content = "Task Cancelled";
            }
            else
            {
                // re-throw any other exception
                throw;
            }
        }
    }
}

private void doWorkThrow(CancellationToken token)
{
    token.ThrowIfCancellationRequested();
    Thread.Sleep(5000);
}
```

Additional reading: ”MSDN Exception Handling (Task Parallel Library)”

Asynchronous Operations

When you want to execute an operation on a separate thread and the thread that initiated the operation, but you don't want to wait for it to complete, then an asynchronous operation is the answer.

.NET Framework 4.5 makes it easier than before to create asynchronous operations; operations that create tasks in the background and coordinate their actions. The **async** keyword lets you create asynchronous operations without blocking the thread and the **await** keyword waits for the result, all in a single method.

The Dispatcher

You can use a **Dispatcher** object to run code on a specific thread. A **Dispatcher** handles a queue containing the thread's work items. One scenario where you want to use a **Dispatcher** is if you run an asynchronous operation that needs to update a WPF UI control; it is not possible to do directly because it runs on a separate thread but with a **Dispatcher** you can achieve it.

The solution is to use the **Dispatcher.BeginInvoke** to within the task logic to queue the update of UI control on the UI thread. The **BeginInvoke** method does not allow anonymous delegates, you need to call an implemented method.

The following code will throw an **InvalidOperationException** exception because the **Label** control is running on the UI thread and the **Task** is running on a parallel thread.

```
private void btnDispatcher_Click(object sender,
RoutedEventArgs e)
{
    Task.Run(() =>
    {
        lblResult.Content = "Not possible";
    });
}
```

To solve this without throwing an exception, you need to use the **Dispatcher.BeginInvoke** method.

```
private void btnDispatcher_Click(object sender,
RoutedEventArgs e)
{
    Task.Run(() =>
    {
        lblResult.Dispatcher.BeginInvoke(
            new Action(() => ChangeUIControls(
                "Text from another thread")));
    });
}

private void ChangeUIControls(string message)
{
    lblResult.Content = message;
}
```

async and await

In .NET Framework 4.5, the **async** and **await** keywords were introduced; they makes it much easier to write asynchronous operations. You use the **await** keyword to suspend execution of the **await** decorated method while a long-running task completes; while the **async** method is suspended, the main thread can continue with its work.

The unique thing about running an asynchronous operation using **async** and **await** is that they enable you to run asynchronous operations on a *single* thread; this makes them especially useful when updating the UI from asynchronous operations.

When executing this code, the UI thread will be blocked until the **Task** has completed.

```
private void btnBLOCKING_UI_THREAD_Click(object sender,
RoutedEventArgs e)
{
    Task<string> task = Task.Run<string>(() =>
    {
        Thread.Sleep(5000);
        return "Finished";
    });

    // Blocks the UI thread until the task has completed.
    lblResult.Content = task.Result;
}
```

To suspend the execution and let the UI thread continues its work, we use the **async** and **await** keywords. Note that the **async** keyword is decorating method header.

```
private async void btnAsyncAndAwait_Click(
object sender, RoutedEventArgs e)
{
    Task<string> task = Task.Run<string>(() =>
    {
        Thread.Sleep(5000);
        return "Finished";
    });

    // Will be called when the Task has a result
    lblResult.Content = await task;
}
```

Additional reading: "Asynchronous Programming with Async and Await (C# and Visual Basic)"

Awaitable Methods

The **await** operator waits on a **Task** to complete in a non-locking manner. An awaitable method should return a **Task** for void methods or a **Task<TResult>** for methods that return a value; one exception is for event methods that can return **void**.

This code shows an implementation of a synchronous method that we will alter to an asynchronous method in the next code sample.

```
private StaticStudent GetDataSynchronous()
{
    var task = Task.Run<StaticStudent>(() =>
    {
        Thread.Sleep(3000);
        return new StaticStudent() {
            FirstName = "Jonas" };
    });

    return task.Result;
}
```

This code shows an implementation of an asynchronous method. Note that both the asynchronous method and the event method have to be decorated with the **async** keyword and that the **await** operator is used in the event method when calling the asynchronous method. The **Content** property of the **Label** will be set when the asynchronous method has completed and the UI thread is not locked while waiting on the asynchronous method to complete.

```
Private async Task<StaticStudent> GetDataAsynchronously()
{
    var task = await Task.Run<StaticStudent>(() =>
    {
        Thread.Sleep(3000);
        return new StaticStudent() {
            FirstName = "Jonas" };
    });
    return task;
}

private async void btnAwaitableMethod_Click(
object sender, RoutedEventArgs e)
{
    var student = await GetDataAsynchronously();
    lblResult.Content = student.FirstName;
}
```

Additional reading: "Async Return Types (C# and Visual Basic)"

Callback methods

You can configure an asynchronous operation to invoke a callback method when it completes its task; the asynchronous method can pass data back to the callback method that processes the information or updates the UI.

A delegate must be created to handle the callback method and it must be passed as a parameter to the asynchronous method. A callback method typically has parameters and returns **void**; this makes the **Action<T>** delegate suitable when declaring a callback method because it can take up to 16 **Type** parameters, **T** is the type you want to return.

In the following sample code, we will fetch a list of students using an asynchronous method and in the callback method we will populate a **ListBox** control.

```
private async void btnCallbackMethod_Click(
object sender, RoutedEventArgs e)
{
    await GetStudents(DisplayStudentsCallback);
}

private  async Task GetStudents(
Action<IEnumerable<StaticStudent>> callback)
{
    var students = await Task.Run(() =>
    {
        SchoolDBEntities context =
            new SchoolDBEntities();
        return (
            from s in context.Students
            select new StaticStudent {
                FirstName = s.FirstName,
                LastName = s.LastName,
                DOB = s.DateOfBirth }).ToList();
    });
```

```
    // Invoke the callback method asynchronously.
    await Task.Run(() => callback(students));
}

private void DisplayStudentsCallback(
IEnumerable<StaticStudent> students)
{
    Dispatcher.BeginInvoke(new Action(() =>
    {
        lstStudents.ItemsSource = students;
        lstStudents.DisplayMemberPath = "FirstName";
    }));
}
```

Additional reading: "Action<T> Delegate"

Asynchronous Programming Model (APM)

.NET Framework supports the APM programming model; it is typically implemented using two methods **Begin*OperationName*** that starts the asynchronous operation and **End*OperationName*** that provides the result. An **IAsyncResult** instance is used to show the status of the asynchronous call. An example of when this APM is used is when making calls to a web service using the **BeginGetResponse** and **EndGetResponse** methods on the **HttpWebRequest** class.

In most cases, you call the **End*OperationName*** within a callback method.

To make it even easier to implement the APM model, you can use the **TaskFactory.FromAsync** method to invoke an asynchronous operation and get the result back in a single line of code. The **TaskFactory.FromAsync** method has overloads that take varying number of arguments.

```
private async void btnAPMModel_Click(object sender,
RoutedEventArgs e)
{
    string url = "http://localhost:57529/
        SchoolDataService.svc/Student";

    HttpWebRequest request =
        (HttpWebRequest)WebRequest.Create(url);

    HttpWebResponse response =
        await Task<WebResponse>.Factory.FromAsync(
        request.BeginGetResponse,
        request.EndGetResponse, request) as
            HttpWebResponse;

    lblResult.Content = String.Format(
        "Returned status code: {0}",
        response.StatusCode);
}
```

Additional reading: "TPL and Traditional .NET Framework Asynchronous Programming"

Exception Handling For Awaitable Methods

Handling exceptions when using the **async** and **await** keywords is easy, you simply use a try/catch block. Exceptions can be handled only when the **await** operator or the **Task.Wait** method are used.

If the joining thread doesn't handle exceptions they will be unobserved and the *.NET Framework Garbage Collector (GC)* usually ignores them; by subscribing to the **TaskScheduler.UnobservedTaskException** you can implement a last resort exception handler.

If you want **GC** to throw unobserved **Task** exceptions, this was the default behavior in .NET Framework versions prior to .NET Framework 4.5, then you set the **ThrowUnobservedTaskExceptions** element to **true** in the **App.Config** file. Any process that contain an unobserved **Task** exception will be terminated.

You could set the **ThrowUnobservedTaskExceptions** element to **true** when developing the application and remove it when you release the code.

```
<configuration>
   <runtime>
       <ThrowUnobservedTaskExceptions enabled="true" />
   </runtime>
</configuration>
```

The following code will throw an exception because the URL is bad.

```
private async void
btnExceptionHandlingForAwait_Click(object sender,
RoutedEventArgs e)
{
   try
   {
       string url = "http://localhost:57529/
           SchoolDataService.svc/NonExisting";

       HttpWebRequest request =
           (HttpWebRequest)WebRequest.Create(url);

       HttpWebResponse response =
           await Task<WebResponse>.Factory.FromAsync(
           request.BeginGetResponse,
           request.EndGetResponse, request) as
               HttpWebResponse;

       lblResult.Content = String.Format(
           "Returned status code: {0}",
           response.StatusCode);
   }
   catch (WebException ex)
   {
       lblResult.Content = "WebException thrown";
   }
}
```

The following code shows how you can implement a last resort exception handler.

```
private void btnLastResortExceptionHandling_Click(
object sender, RoutedEventArgs e)
{
    string url = "http://localhost:57529/
        SchoolDataService.svc/NonExisting";

    TaskScheduler.UnobservedTaskException += (object s,
        UnobservedTaskExceptionEventArgs eArg) =>
    {
        foreach (Exception ex in
        ((AggregateException)eArg.Exception)
        .InnerExceptions)
        {
            lblResult.Dispatcher.BeginInvoke(
                new Action(() =>
                ChangeUIControls("Exception thrown")));
        }

        eArg.SetObserved();
    };

    // Launch a task that will throw an unobserved
    // exception due to an invalid URL.
    Task.Run(() =>
    {
        using (WebClient client = new WebClient())
        {
            client.DownloadStringTaskAsync(url);
        }
    });

    Thread.Sleep(3000);
    GC.WaitForPendingFinalizers();
    GC.Collect();
}
```

Synchronizing Concurrent Data Access

Responsiveness and performance are two benefits of multitasking, but there are challenges as well. One of them is concurrent data access; if two resources update the same data problem can arise leaving the data in an unpredictable state.

To solve these challenges, you can use locking mechanisms and concurrent collections.

Lock Block

If multiple threads access the same data simultaneously, there is a risk of corrupt data being used and stored. Let's say you have a warehouse application that has different methods that updates and checks the stock level of an item. If the stock level is being updated by one thread when a request for the current stock level, then there is a chance that the request is being made before the update to the stock level has completed.

The solution is to use a **Lock** block to implement mutual-exclusion locks where critical updates are made; a lock of this type will lockout any other threads than the one that are currently holding the lock. Use the following syntax to implement a lock: **lock** *(object) {statement block}*. The *object* in the lock should be declared as private in the class and serve only one purpose, to hold the lock with something that is unique. Write the critical code within the *statement block*.

The following code shows the class that has the method with the lock.

```
private class Warehouse
{
    private object stockLock = new object();
    int stock;
```

```
    public Warehouse(int initialStock)
    {
        stock = initialStock;
    }

    public int GetStockLevel()
    {
        return stock;
    }

    public bool FetchItemsFromStorage(int soldItems)
    {
        lock (stockLock)
        {
            if (stock >= soldItems)
            {
                Thread.Sleep(3000);
                // Calculate new stock level
                stock = stock - soldItems;
                return true;
            }
            else
            {
                // Insufficient stock available
                return false;
            }
        }
    }
}
```

The following code shows the class that calls to the method with the lock implemented. If both buttons are clicked in sequence then the second call will have to wait for the first call to end. To be able to click both buttons we have to run the cals on separate threads hence the **async** and **await** keywords.

If we executed this code with the lock, we would get the following result: firstUpdateTask = true, firstStockLevelCountTask = 1, second-UpdateTask = false, secondStockLevelCountTask = 1.

If we removed the lock and executed this code, we would get the following result: firstUpdateTask = true, firstStockLevelCountTask = 1, secondUpdateTask = true, secondStockLevelCountTask = -2. The second call yields corrupt data because the stock level updates was not locked and could be executed simultaneously with the first call.

```
Warehouse w = new Warehouse(4);
bool firstUpdateTask, secondUpdateTask;
int firstStockLevelCountTask, secondStockLevelCountTask;

private async void
ConcurrentAccessToDataWithLock_Click(object sender,
RoutedEventArgs e)
{
    firstUpdateTask = await Task.Run<bool>(() =>
        w.FetchItemsFromStorage(3));
    firstStockLevelCountTask = await Task.Run<int>(() =>
        w.GetStockLevel());
}

private async void
ConcurrentAccessToDataUpdateStockLevelWithLock_Click(
object sender, RoutedEventArgs e)
{
    secondUpdateTask = await Task.Run<bool>(() =>
        w.FetchItemsFromStorage(3));
    secondStockLevelCountTask = await Task.Run<int>(() =>
        w.GetStockLevel());
}
```

Additional reading: "lock Statement (C# Reference)" and "Thread Synchronization (C# and Visual Basic)"

Synchronization Primitives

Synchronization of threads is handled by the .NET Framework though synchronization primitive mechanisms. The most frequently used are the ManualResetEventSlim class that makes it possible for one or more threads to wait for an event to finish; only one thread can access the resource at any one time. The SemaphoreSlim class can be used to restrict one or more resources to a limited number of concurrent threads. You can have an event wait until a fixed number of threads have finished by using the CountdownEvent class. To restrict reading and writing to a resource you can use the ReaderWriterLockSlim class to allow multiple threads to read but only one thread to write to the resource. If you need multiple threads to reach a certain point before continuing you can use the Barrier class to temporarily halt execution of threads.

Additional Reading:

"ManualResetEventSlim Class", "SemaphoreSlim Class"

"CountdownEvent Class", "ReaderWriterLockSlim Class"

"Barrier Class"

Concurrent Collections

When using Tasks or other multi-threading techniques, you must ensure that the collections you use are thread-safe, which standard collections are not. There are several thread-safe collections that you can utilize when building a multi-threaded application. The reason you need thread safe collections is to keep the integrity of the data intact; no two resources should be able to use the same data simultaneously and cause corrupt data. You find the thread-safe collections in the **System .Collections.Concurrent** namespace.

Thread-safe Collections

These collections are designed to work in a thread-safe manner in a multi-threaded application.

- **ConcurrentBag<T>**
  Stores an unordered collection of items.
- **ConcurrentDictionary<TKey, TValue>**
  Stores a collection of dictionary items using key-value pairs.
- **ConcurrentQueue<T>**
  Works the same way as the **Queue<T>** class.

- **ConcurrentStack<T>**
  Works the same way as the **Stack<T>** class.
- **BlockingCollection<T>**
  Is a wrapper for the **IProducerConsumerCollection<T>** interface. It can block read requests until a read lock is available. It can block items being added to the underlying collection until space is available.
- **IProducerConsumerCollection<T>**
  This interface defines methods that are implemented by classes that distinguish between producers that add items and consumers that read items. The interface is implemented by the **ConcurrentBag<T>**, **ConcurrentQueue<T>** and **ConcurrentStack<T>** collections.

This sample code shows how you can implement a thread-safe **ConcurrentQueue** and **ConcurrentBag**. When we click the button, orders will begin pouring in to the queue and will begin being processed by one of three people. When all processing is done, we present the result in a **ListBox**.

```
ConcurrentQueue<string> queue = new
ConcurrentQueue<string>();
ConcurrentBag<Order> orders = new ConcurrentBag<Order>();

class Order
{
    public Order(string name, string description)
    { Name = name; Description = description; }
    public string Name { get; set; }
    public string Description { get; set; }
    public int Id {
        get
        {
            return Convert.ToInt32(
                Description.Substring(5));
        }
    }
}
```

```
private void PlaceOrders()
{
    for (int i = 1; i <= 25; i++)
    {
        Thread.Sleep(5);
        String order = String.Format("Order {0}", i);
        queue.Enqueue(order);
    }
}

private void ProcessOrders(string name)
{
    string order;
    while (true) //continue indefinitely
        if (queue.TryDequeue(out order))
            orders.Add(new Order(name, order));
}

private void ConcurrentQueue_Click(object sender,
RoutedEventArgs e)
{
    var taskPlaceOrders = Task.Run(() => PlaceOrders());

    Task.Run(() => ProcessOrders("Carl"));
    Task.Run(() => ProcessOrders("Lisa"));
    Task.Run(() => ProcessOrders("Mary"));

    taskPlaceOrders.Wait();

    lstOrders.ItemsSource =
        from o in orders
        orderby o.Id ascending
        select String.Format("{0} processed by {1}",
            o.Description, o.Name);
}
```

Additional reading: "System.Collections.Concurrent Namespace"

Calling Unmanaged Code

Sometimes you want your application to interact with other systems such as *Component Object Model (COM)* objects and unmanaged C++ components; to call into unmanaged code you use the *Dynamic Language Runtime (DLR)*. The ability to call COM objects means that you canreuse old components that are written in other languages and that already exist in your organization.

Dynamic Objects

Normally when declaring variables in C#, you specify the type of that variable. If you try to call a method that is not in that type, you get a compilation error. In cases when you want or need to use dynamic variables that are not bound to the static variable declaration of C# you can use dynamic objects that are not checked until run-time. You mainly use dynamic objects to call dynamic languages and unmanaged code.

Dynamic languages such as IronPython and IronRuby have the benefits of not needing to be built or compiled, which means faster development cycles. They are more flexible in the sense that they don't have static types to handle and you don't have to learn a strongly typed object model.

One of the drawbacks of dynamic languages is that they have slower execution times because there are no optimization steps taken during the build process.

Unmanaged code has the benefit of being very flexible and generally execution times are faster than managed execution times. Two common scenarios where you want to call COM objects are either when you want to reuse existing components in your organization or you need to call some functionality in the operating system.

Reusing functionality from other technologies such as COM, C++, Microsoft AcitveX and Microsoft Win32 APIs is called *interoperability*.

Additional reading: "DynamicObject Class"

The DLR waits with type-safety checking until run-time, the opposite of the *Common Language Runtime (CLR)* which checks at compile time and is used for managed code. The DLR also abstracts away the details of interoperating with unmanaged components; it even handles the conversion of types between the two environments. It is not language specific and handles marshaling of data between the different environments such as IronPython and the .NET Framework. Al- type checking and checking that method signatures exist in the objects are done at run-time.

Additional reading: "Dynamic Language Runtime Overview"

Use the **dynamic** keyword when you want to create a dynamic object. Using the dynamic keyword reduces the amount of code you have to write compared to the traditional way of consuming a COM component because you no longer have to pass in **Type.Missing** for optional parameters and don't have to use the **ref** keyword.

Be aware that the following implications exist when using dynamic objects.

- The variable will be created with the **object** type and type checking will be done at run-time.
- The compiler will not perform any type checking of dynamic code.
- The *IntelliSense* feature will not work for dynamic objects.

Additional reading: "Using Type dynamic (C# Programming Guide)"

In this example, we will create a Microsoft Excel workbook using a **dynamic** object and the **Application** class in the **Microsoft.Office .Interop.Excel** COM component; you need to set a reference to the .NET assembly with the same name.

```
using excel = Microsoft.Office.Interop.Excel;
string filePath = "C:\\Sample Files\\school.xlsx";
private void btnCreateExcelApplication_Click(
object sender, RoutedEventArgs e)
{
    dynamic excelApp = new excel.Application();
    excelApp.Visible = true;
    excelApp.Workbooks.Add();

    excel._Worksheet workSheet =
        (excel.Worksheet)excelApp.ActiveSheet;
    workSheet.Cells[1, "A"] = "First name";
    workSheet.Cells[1, "B"] = "Last name";
    workSheet.Cells[1, "C"] = "DOB";

    SchoolDBEntities school = new SchoolDBEntities();
    int row = 2;
    foreach(var student in school.Students)
    {
        workSheet.Cells[row, "A"] = student.FirstName;
        workSheet.Cells[row, "B"] = student.LastName;
        workSheet.Cells[row, "C"] = student.DateOfBirth;
        row++;
    };

    workSheet.Columns[1].AutoFit();
    workSheet.Columns[2].AutoFit();
    workSheet.Columns[3].AutoFit();
    book.SaveAs(filePath);
}
```

This sample code shows how to open a saved Excel workbook.

```
using excel = Microsoft.Office.Interop.Excel;
string filePath = "C:\\Sample Files\\school.xlsx";
private void btnOpenExcelWorkbook_Click(object sender,
RoutedEventArgs e)
{
    dynamic excelApp = new excel.Application();
    dynamic book = excelApp.Workbooks.Open(filePath);
    excelApp.Visible = true;
}
```

Additional reading: "How to: Define and Execute Dynamic Methods"

Garbage Collection (GC)

When working with unmanaged resources it is important to know how release these resources when they are no longer used.

Managed objects are created by the CLR at run-rime when the new keyword is used this is done in two steps; first enough memory is allocated for the object on the Heap and then the memory is initialized to the new object.

When an object is destroyed, when it goes out of scope or the reference is dropped, then the CLR use the *Garbage Collector (GC)* to clean up the object. This is done in two steps where the first is to release the resource and then reclaim the memory that was allocated for the object.

GC runs automatically in the background and handles any objects that no longer have references to them. You can manually start **GC** by calling the **GC.Collect** method; be aware that this can slow down the system temporarily as the **GC** goes through the object tree that keeps track of all created objects.

Additional reading: "Garbage Collection C#"

Dispose Pattern

.NET Framework uses a dispose pattern to free resources, this is especially important when using *unmanaged resources*. To implement a dispose pattern, you implement the **IDisposable** interface that resides in the **System** namespace; the interface contains a single method **Dispose** where you place all clean-up code. Call the **Dispose** method when destroying an object, making sure that the resources the object hold are reclaimed before the actual object is reclaimed by the **GC**.

When creating managed wrapper classes for unmanaged resources, you should implement the **IDisposable** pattern. Consider implementing an overloaded **Dispose** method that takes a **Boolean** parameter stating if managed resources should be disposed by the method. After the **Dispose** method has been called, the **GC.SuppressFinalize** method should be called to instruct the **GC** that the object already has been released and **GC** can skip the finalizing code.

You can implement a *destructor* in the class that cleans up the object and calls the **Dispose** method as part of the **GC** clean-up. The destructor method name always begins with a tilde (~) sign followed by the name of the class and it has no scope defined. The destructor is automatically converted into an override of the **Finalize** method.

Additional reading: "IDisposable Interface"

The following sample code show how to implement the **IDisposable** pattern in a class.

```
class DisposePattern : IDisposable
{
    bool _isDisposed;

    protected virtual void Dispose(
    bool disposeManagedResources)
    {
        if (this._isDisposed) return;

        if (disposeManagedResources)
        {
            // Release managed resources here
        }

        // Release unmanaged resources here;
        // unmanaged resource should always be released

        // Set the _isDisposed to indicate that the
        // object already has been disposed
        this._isDisposed = true;
    }

    public void Dispose()
    {
        Dispose(true);
        GC.SuppressFinalize(this);
    }

    // The destructor is called by GC unless we have
    // called the Dispose method manually and the
    // GC.SuppressFinalize method has been called
    ~DisposePattern()
    {
        Dispose(false);
    }
```

```
    public void DoSomeWork()
    {
        if (this._isDisposed)
            throw new ObjectDisposedException(
                String.Format(
                "{0} Has already been disposed",
                this.GetType().Name));
    }
}
```

Manually Disposing an Object

The following sample code show how to use the **Dispose** method on an object of the class implementing the **IDisposable** pattern. Calling the **Dispose** method manually will tell **GC** that it does not have to handle the finalization of the object; this can speed up the reclaiming of the allocated memory of the object. It is good practice to check that the object is not null before calling the **Dispose** method.

```
class TestDisposePattern
{
    public TestDisposePattern()
    {
        var disposePattern = new DisposePattern();
        try
        {
            disposePattern.DoSomeWork();
        }
        finally
        {
            if (disposePattern != null)
                disposePattern.Dispose();
        }
    }
}
```

You also can use a **using** statement to implicitly invoke the **Dispose** method when the code in the using block has finished executing. This approach is exception-safe meaning that the **GC** will dispose of the objects even if an exception is thrown within the **using** block.

```
class TestDisposePattern
{
    public TestDisposePattern()
    {
        using (var theObject = default(DisposePattern))
        {
            theObject.DoSomeWork();
        }
    }
}
```

Additional reading: "using Statement (C# Reference)"

Reflection

Reuse of code and components is something you always want to keep in mind when building an application. Reflection is a way to use existing assemblies in your application and to inspect their metadata at run time; just keep in mind that it is marginally slower than static C# code. Use the classes in the **System.Reflection** namespace to implement reflection in your applications.

An example of where reflection is used is the **System.Runtime.Serialization** namespace that uses reflection to determine which type members to serialize.

You can examine a third-party assembly with unknown types and members to see if your application satisfies the dependencies of the assembly. In some cases, such as if you are implementing a generic storage repository; you might want to use reflection to inspect each type and its attributes before storing it. In other cases, you might want to have pluggable assemblies that load at run-time. One way to implement it is to look for specific interfaces with reflection. If you are building a virtualized platform that uses types and methods created in a language such as JavaScript you might want to define and execute methods at run-time.

Apart from the reflection classes listed below. you also might find the **System.Type** class useful when implementing reflection; one method of particular interest is the **GetFields** method that fetches the fields defined within the type in a list of **FieldInfo** objects.

This is a list of some of the classes in the **System.Reflection** namespace.

- **Assembly**
  Use this class to inspect an assembly's metadata and types, and to load an assembly.
- **TypeInfo**
  Use this class to inspect a type's characteristics.
- **ParameterInfo**
  Use this class to inspect what parameters a member takes.
- **ConstructorInfo**
  Use this class to inspect a type's constructor.
- **FieldInfo**
  Use this class to inspect the fields' characteristics of a type.
- **MemeberInfo**
  Use this class to inspect the members exposed by a type.
- **PropertyInfo**
  Use this class to inspect the properties characteristics of a type.
- **MethodInfo**
  Use this class to inspect the methods characteristics of a type.

Additional reading: "MSDN Type Class" and "Reflection in the .NET Framework"

Loading Assemblies

The **Assembly** class of the **System.Reflection** namespace has two contexts; one that is for reflection-only operations that you can use to examine the assembly metadata, using static methods, but not execute any code. The other is the execution context that you use to execute an assembly that has been loaded.

Trying to execute an assembly using the reflection-only context will result in an **InvalidOperationException** exception being thrown. This context is faster than the execution context.

The **Assembly** class contains the following **static** methods for loading an assembly at run time.

- **LoadFrom**
  Use an absolute file path to load an assembly in *execution context.*
- **ReflectionOnlyLoad**
  Will load an assembly into a binary BLOB object using a *reflection-only context.*
- **ReflectionOnlyLoadFrom**
  Use an absolute file path to load an assembly in *reflection-only context.*

When the assembly is loaded, you can use the following methods and properties to inspect and execute it.

- **FullName**
  Retrieves the full name of the assembly that contains the assembly version and public key token.
- **GetReferencedAssemblies**
  Fetches a list of all the names of the assemblies that the loaded assembly references.
- **GlobalAssemblyCache**
  States if the assembly was loaded from the GAC.
- **Location**
  The absolute path to the assembly file.
- **ReflectionOnly**
  States if the assembly was loaded using a *reflection-only context.*

- **GetType**
  Fetches an instance of a Type in the assembly with the type name.
- **GetTypes**
  Fetches an array of all the types in the assembly; the array elements are represented by the **Type** type.

Additional reading: "Assembly Class"

The following code sample shows the three ways of loading an assembly; you only have to use one of them when implementing your solution.

```
class ReflectionClass
{
    string assemblyPath =
        @"C:\Sample Files\TestAssembly.dll";

    private Assembly LoadExecutableAssembly()
    {
        // Execute context
        var assembly = Assembly.LoadFrom(assemblyPath);

        return assembly;
    }

    private Assembly LoadReflectionAssemblyBLOB()
    {
        // Reflection-only context - BLOB
        var rawBytes = File.ReadAllBytes(assemblyPath);
        var reflectionOnlyAssembly =
            Assembly.ReflectionOnlyLoad(rawBytes);

        return reflectionOnlyAssembly;
    }
```

```
    private Assembly LoadReflectionAssembly()
    {
        // Reflection-only context
        var reflectionOnlyLoadFromAssembly =
            Assembly.ReflectionOnlyLoadFrom(
                assemblyPath);

        return reflectionOnlyLoadFromAssembly;
    }
}
```

Examining Types

With reflection you can examine an assembly fetching information about individual members or all members of a type.

The following code samples build on the code in the previous example; add the methods to the same class.

The following code shows a static class with an extension method that is called to print the results from the method calls and an example of how to use the extension method.

```
public static class Extensions
{
    public static void Print(this IList<string> list)
    {
        foreach (var item in list)
            Console.WriteLine(item);
    }
}

class ReflectionClass
{
    public ReflectionClass()
    {
        GetFields().Print();
    }
}
```

GetType/GetTypes

Use the GetType method to fetch a type in an assembly by its fully qualified name, null will be returned if the type does not exist. Use the **GetTypes** method to fetch all types in an array of Type objects.

```
private IList<string> GetAssemblyTypes()
{
    var assembly = LoadReflectionAssembly();

    return (from t in assembly.GetTypes()
        select t.FullName).ToList();
}

private Type GetAssemblyType()
{
    var assembly = LoadReflectionAssembly();

    return assembly.GetType("TestAssembly.MyClass");
}
```

GetConstructors

Use the **GetConstructors** method to fetch all constructors of a type; it returns an array of **ConstructorInfo** objects. Use the **GetParameters** method to get the parameters of each constructor.

```
private IList<string> GetConstructorParameters()
{
    List<string> result = new List<string>();

    var type = GetAssemblyType();
    foreach (var constructor in type.GetConstructors())
    {
        result.Add(String.Format(
            "Constructor: {0}", type.Name));

        if(constructor.GetParameters().Count() == 0)
            result.Add("    -> No parameters available");
```

```
        foreach (var parameter in
            constructor.GetParameters())
                result.Add(String.Format(
                    "    -> Parameter: {0}",
                    parameter.Name));
    }

    return result;
}
```

GetFields

Use the **GetFields** method to fetch all fields of a type; it returns an array of **FieldInfo** objects. Use the **BindingFlags** collection to select which fields are to be fetched. The fields will be listed on the form *[private/ public] Fieldname*.

```
private IList<string> GetFields()
{
    var type = GetAssemblyType();

    return (
        from t in type.GetFields(BindingFlags.Instance |
            BindingFlags.NonPublic | BindingFlags.Public)
        where !t.Name.Contains("<")
        select String.Format("{0} {1}", t.IsPrivate ?
            "private" : "public", t.Name)
    ).ToList();
}
```

GetProperties

Use the **GetProperties** method to fetch all fields of a type; it returns an array of **PropertyInfo** objects. Use the **BindingFlags** collection to select which properties are to be fetched. The properties will be listed on the form *[private/public] Propertyname {[public/private] get; [public/ private] set;}*. The **GetMethod.IsPrivate** property states if the property is public or private and the **GetGetMethod.IsPrivate** and **GetSetMethod .IsPrivate** property states if the property's getter and setter blocks are public or private.

```
private IList<string> GetProperties()
{
    var type = GetAssemblyType();

    return (
        from t in type.GetProperties(
            BindingFlags.Instance |
            BindingFlags.NonPublic |
            BindingFlags.Public)
        select String.Format(
            "{0} {1} {{ {2} get; {3} set; }}",
            t.GetMethod.IsPrivate ? "private" : "public",
            t.ToString(),
            t.GetGetMethod(true).IsPrivate ?
                "private" : "public",
            t.GetSetMethod(true).IsPrivate ?
                "private" : "public")
    ).ToList();
}
```

GetMethods

Use the **GetMethods** method to fetch all methods of a type; it returns an array of **MethodInfo** objects. Use the **BindingFlags** collection to select which methods are to be fetched. The methods will be listed on the form *[private/public] Methodname*.

```
private IList<string> GetMethods()
{
    var type = GetAssemblyType();

    return (from t in type.GetMethods(
        BindingFlags.Instance |
        BindingFlags.NonPublic |
        BindingFlags.Public)
    select String.Format("{0} {1}", t.IsPrivate ?
        "private" : "public", t.Name)).ToList();
}
```

GetMembers

Use the **GetMembers** method to fetch all members of a type; it returns an array of **MemberInfo** objects. Use the **BindingFlags** collection to select which members are to be fetched. The members will be listed on the form *MemeberType DataType Membername*. Use the **MemberType** property to find out what type the current member has. In the *Method* case, we remove the property *get_* and *set_* methods because the properties will be listed in the *Properties* case.

```
private IList<string> GetMembers()
{
    List<string> result = new List<string>();
    var type = GetAssemblyType();

    foreach (var m in type.GetMembers(
    BindingFlags.Instance | BindingFlags.NonPublic |
    BindingFlags.Public))
    {
        switch (m.MemberType)
        {
            case MemberTypes.Method:
                if(!m.Name.Contains("get_") &&
                !m.Name.Contains("set_"))
                    result.Add(String.Format(
                        "{0, -10}{1}",
                        MemberTypes.Method.ToString(),
                        m.ToString()));
                break;
            case MemberTypes.Property:
                result.Add(String.Format(
                    "{0, -10}{1}",
                    MemberTypes.Property.ToString(),
                    m.ToString()));
                break;
        }
    }
    return result;
}
```

Invoking Members

In .NET you can invoke objects using reflection which is done in the same basic way as with regular instantiations using C#; you first create an instance of the type then you call methods and use properties.

If you are using static members, there is no need to create an instance explicitly when using reflection.

We will use a class named **Student** from the assembly named *Test-Assembly.dll*, and the following code will be the set-up for coming examples.

```
public partial class Student
{
    public int Id { get; set; }
    public string FirstName { get; set; }
    public string LastName { get; set; }
    public DateTime DateOfBirth { get; private set; }
    public static string School { get; set; }

    public Student()
    {
        DateOfBirth = DateTime.MinValue;
    }

    public Student(DateTime dateOfBirth)
    {
        DateOfBirth = dateOfBirth;
    }

    public int GetAge()
    {
        TimeSpan difference =
            DateTime.Now.Subtract(DateOfBirth);

        int ageInYears = (int)(difference.Days / 365.25);
        return ageInYears;
    }
```

```
public int GetAge(DateTime dateOfBirth)
    {
        if (DateOfBirth == DateTime.MinValue ||
dateOfBirth != DateOfBirth)
            DateOfBirth = dateOfBirth;

        return GetAge();
    }
}
```

Creating an Instance of a Type

To create an instance of **Type,** you use the **GetType** method on the assembly that you have loaded with the **LoadFrom** method of the **Assembly** class. When you have the Type loaded, you can use the **GetConstructor** method to fetch the desired constructor; matching the parameter signature with the array of **Types** that you pass in to the **GetConstructor** method, to get the default constructor, you pass in an empty array of length zero (0).

This sample code shows how you create an instance of a **Type** in an assembly loaded with reflection.

```
class ReflectionClass
{
    string assemblyPath =
        @"C:\Sample Files\TestAssembly.dll";

    private Assembly LoadExecutableAssembly()
    {
        // Execute context
        var assembly = Assembly.LoadFrom(assemblyPath);
        return assembly;
    }

    private Type GetExecutableAssemblyType()
    {
        var assembly = LoadExecutableAssembly();
        return assembly.GetType("TestAssembly.Student");
    }
```

```
    private void CreateInstanceDefaultConstructor()
    {
        var type = GetExecutableAssemblyType();
        var constructor = type.GetConstructor(
            new Type[0]);
        instance = constructor.Invoke(new object[0]);
    }

    private void CreateInstance()
    {
        var type = GetExecutableAssemblyType();
        var constructor = type.GetConstructor(
            new Type[1]{ typeof(DateTime) });
        instance = constructor.Invoke(new object[1]{
            new DateTime(1970, 5, 4) });
    }
}
```

Calling Methods

To call a method on a type in an assembly using reflection, you call the **GetMethod** method on the instance **Type** (use the **GetType** method), then call the **Invoke** method on the **MethodInfo** object returned from the **GetMethod** method; pass in the **Type** instance and the list of argument (as an object array), if the method takes no parameters then pass in an empty object array.

This sample code shows how you call a method using reflection.

```
private int ExecuteMethod()
{
    var method = instance.GetType().GetMethod(
        "GetAge", new Type[0]);

    var age = method.Invoke(instance, new object[0]);
    return Convert.ToInt32(age);
}
```

Setting Property Values

To assign a value to an instance property using reflection, you first have to fetch the property from the instance **Type** using the **GetProperty** method; you can then use the **SetValue** method on the **PropertyInfo** object returned from the **GetProperty** method to set the value of the property.

This sample code shows how you assign a value to an instance property using reflection.

```
private void SetPropertyValue(string propertyName,
object value)
{
    var property = instance.GetType().GetProperty(
        propertyName);
    property.SetValue(instance, value);
}
```

To assign a value to a **static** property using reflection, you first have to fetch the property from the **Type** using the **GetProperty** method, no instance is needed. You can then use the **SetValue** method on the **PropertyInfo** object returned from the **GetProperty** method to set the value of the property.

This sample code shows how you assign a value to a **static** property using reflection.

```
private void SetStaticPropertyValue(string propertyName,
object value)
{
    var type = GetExecutableAssemblyType();
    var property = type.GetProperty(propertyName);
    property.SetValue(null, value);
}
```

Getting Property Values

To fetch a value from an instance property using reflection, you first have to fetch the property from the instance **Type** using the **GetProperty** method; you can then use the **GetValue** method on the **PropertyInfo** object returned from the **GetProperty** method to get the value of the property.

This sample code shows how you fetch a value from an instance property using reflection.

```
private string GetPropertyValue(string propertyName)
{
    var property = instance.GetType().GetProperty(
        propertyName);
    var value = property.GetValue(instance);
    return value.ToString();
}
```

To fetch a value from a static property using reflection you first have to fetch the property from the Type using the **GetProperty** method, no instance is needed; you can then use the GetValue method on the **PropertyInfo** object returned from the GetProperty method to set the value of the property.

This sample code shows how you fetch a value from a **static** property using reflection.

```
private string GetStaticPropertyValue(
string propertyName)
{
    var type = GetExecutableAssemblyType();
    var property = type.GetProperty(propertyName);
    var value = property.GetValue(null);
    return value.ToString();
}
```

Custom Attributes

Custom attributes can be used to add metadata to a **Type** or a member; you can then use reflection to read that metadata at run-time. The application can use the information that attributes provide to control the behavior of the application. Attributes also can be used to aid developers in the development process. The abstract **Attribute** class is the base class of all attributes.

In earlier chapters, we have used attributes directly or indirectly that the .NET Framework provides such as **Serializable, NonSerialized** and **DataContract**. Other important attributes are **Obsolete** that states that the Type or member has been suspended and is only available for backwards compatibility; **QueryInterceptor,** which can be used to handle access to an entity in WCF Data Services; and **ConfigurationProperty** that can be used to map a property to a section in an application configuration file.

To apply an attribute, you need to add a using statement to the namespace that holds the attribute. Then you can apply the attribute to the **Type** or member passing in all necessary parameters that the attribute constructor requires; ID named parameters are used to assign values to those.

This sample code shows how you apply an attribute to a property.

```
public partial class Student
{
    ...
    [Obsolete("This property is obsolete and will
        be replaced by a SchoolId in the next
        release.", true)]
    public static string School { get; set; }
}
```

Additional reading: "Attribute Class"

Creating a Custom Attribute

Custom attributes that you create work the same way built in attributes do.

To create a custom attribute, the class that will be used to define the attribute must derive from the **Attribute** class or another attribute class. Decorate the class with the **AttributeUsage** attribute to the element types that it will be applied to. Define a constructor that takes the necessary parameters that you want the attribute to hold values for. Any properties that have a **get** accessor are in the class will be exposed as named parameters.

If you want the possibility to use the attribute several times on a **Type** or a member, then you have to set the **AllowMultiple** argument of the **AttributeUsage** attribute; otherwise, you don't have to add the **AllowMultiple** argument.

This sample code shows how you create a custom attribute.

```
[AttributeUsage(AttributeTargets.All,
AllowMultiple = true)]
class DeveloperAttribute : Attribute
{
    string _name, _revision;

    public string Name { get { return _name; } }
    public string revision { get { return _revision; } }

    public DeveloperAttribute(string name,
    string revision)
    {
        _name = name;
        _revision = revision;
    }
```

```
    public override string ToString()
    {
        return "Name: " + _name +
            " --- Revision: " + _revision;
    }
}
```

This sample code shows how you use a custom attribute.

```
[Developer("Jonas", "1.2.3")]
class UseAttributes
{
    [Developer("Jonas", "3.2.1")]
    public void DoSomeWork() { }
}
```

Additional reading: "Creating Custom Attributes (C# and Visual Basic)"

Attribute and Reflection

You can use reflection to fetch the metadata that you or your team has added with attributes. Use the extension methods of the **System .Reflection** class to access attribute metadata.

This sample code shows how you fetch a custom attribute from a type in the executing assembly using reflection. The **getInheritedAttributes** parameter specifies whether inherited attributes should be included.

```
private string GetSpecificTypeAttribute(
bool getInheritedAttributes)
{
    var assembly = Assembly.GetExecutingAssembly();
    var type = assembly.GetType(
        "Samples.Samples.UseSingleAttribute");
    var attribute = type.GetCustomAttribute(
        typeof(DeveloperAttribute),
        getInheritedAttributes);

    return attribute.ToString();
}
```

This sample code shows how you fetch a custom attribute, even if it has been used multiple times or if different attributes have been used on the same **Type**, from a **Type** in the executing assembly using reflection. The **getInheritedAttributes** parameter specifies whether inherited attributes should be included.

```
private List<string> GetTypeAttributes(bool
getInheritedAttributes)
{
    var assembly = Assembly.GetExecutingAssembly();
    var type = assembly.GetType(
        "Samples.Samples.UseAttributes");
    var attributes = type.GetCustomAttributes(
        typeof(DeveloperAttribute),
        getInheritedAttributes);

    return (from a in attributes
        select a.ToString()).ToList();
}
```

This sample code shows how you fetch custom attributes from a method in a **Type** in the executing assembly using reflection. Note the alternate way to use the **GetCustomAttributes** method.

```
private List<string> GetMethodAttributes(
bool inheritedAttributes)
{
    var assembly = Assembly.GetExecutingAssembly();
    var type = assembly.GetType(
        "Samples.Samples.UseAttributes");
    var method = type.GetMethod("DoSomeWork");
    var attributes = method.GetCustomAttributes
        <DeveloperAttribute>(inheritedAttributes);

    return (
        from a in attributes
        select "From Method -> " + a.ToString()
    ).ToList();
}
```

Additional reading: "Accessing Custom Attributes"

CodeDOM – Dynamically Generate Managed Code

Sometimes the project requires that you create code at run-time; to achieve this, you can use the CodeDOM that .NET Framework defines.

The CodeDOM can generate code from a model that you build at run-time using one of the generators provided for C#, VB.NET and Java-Script.

You can use the CodeDOM to generate code files that you can compile into applications at run-time. There are a few namespaces that you need to use: *System.CodeDom* which is used to define a code model; *System.CodeDom.Compiler* is used to generate the code files, and the code compiler for the language of choice *Microsoft.CSharp.CSharpCode-Provider*, *Microsoft.VisualBasic.VBCodeProvider*, and *Microsoft.Java-Script.JscriptCodeProvider*.

The following classes can be used when creating a model with the *System.CodeDom* namespace. Once the model is complete, you use one of the previously mentioned providers to generate the code.

- **CodeCompileUnit**
  Use this to create a collection of **Types** that will be compiled into an assembly.
- **CodeNamespace**
  Use this to create namespaces in the assembly.
- **CodeTypeDeclaration**
  Use this to create a class, structure, enumeration or interface.
- **CodeMemeberMethod**
  Use this to create a method and add it to a **Type**.

- **CodeMemeberField**
  Use this to create a field (variable) such as **bool** or **int** and add it to a **Type**.
- **CodeMemeberProperty**
  Use this to create a property and add it to a **Type**.
- **CodeConstructor**
  Use this to create a constructor method that enables you to create an instance of the **Type**.
- **CodeTypeConstructor**
  Use this to create a static constructor that enables you to create a singleton **Type**.
- **CodeEntryPoint**
  Use this to create an entry point which normally is a **static** method called **Main**.
- **CodeMethodInvokeExpression**
  Is used to represent a set of instructions that can be executed.
- **CodeMethodReferenceExpression**
  Is typically used when defining the body of a method to create a reference type that you want to use.
- **CodePrimitiveExpression**
  Defines an expression value that you can store in a field or use as a method parameter.

Additional reading: "Dynamic Source Code Generation and Compilation"

Types and Members

You use the same pattern when creating a **Type** using the *CodeDOM* as you would when using regular code, the difference is that you define it as instructions that the *CodeDOM* can interpret.

The End Result

The following sample shows the compiled **Type** that we will be creating, saving into a C# file named *Program.cs* and compile into an application.

```
Namespace Samples.Dynamic
{
    using System;
    public class Program
    {
        public static void Main()
        {
            Console.WriteLine(
                "-> My dynamic message <-");
            Console.ReadLine();
        }
    }
}
```

The Type and Member Creation

The following sample code shows how to create a class containing an entry point method named Main that writes some text to the **Console** window.

First, we create unit that will hold the type and add the *System.Dynamic* namespace to it, then we add a using statement for the *System* namespace, declare that it is a *Program* we are creating and add an entry point method named Main using the **CodeEntryPointMethod** class.

Once the unit is defined, we continue by adding two method calls to the **WriteLine** and **ReadLine Console** methods. The last thing we do is to return the unit from the method.

```
private CodeCompileUnit CreateTypeAndMemebers()
{
    var unit = new CodeCompileUnit();
    var dynamicNamespace =
        new CodeNamespace("Samples.Dynamic");

    unit.Namespaces.Add(dynamicNamespace);
```

```
    dynamicNamespace.Imports.Add(
        new CodeNamespaceImport("System"));
    var programType = new CodeTypeDeclaration("Program");
    dynamicNamespace.Types.Add(programType);
    var mainMethod = new CodeEntryPointMethod();
    programType.Members.Add(mainMethod);

    var writeLine = new CodeMethodInvokeExpression(
        new CodeTypeReferenceExpression("Console"),
        "WriteLine", new CodePrimitiveExpression(
        "-> My dynamic message <-"));
    mainMethod.Statements.Add(writeLine);

    var readLine = new CodeMethodInvokeExpression(
        new CodeTypeReferenceExpression("Console"),
        "ReadLine", new CodePrimitiveExpression[0]);
    mainMethod.Statements.Add(readLine);

    return unit;
}
```

Additional reading: "Using the CodeDOM"

Compiling a CodeDOM model

After defining a model, you can compile it into a source code file (.cs for C# code); this file can then be compiled into an executable assembly.

The following sample code shows how you can compile the model into a .cs file named *Program.cs*.

First, we create a C# provider using the **CSharpCodeProvider** class that will generate the C# file, then we create an instance of the **StreamWriter** class that we will use to write the model to the file using an instance of the **IndentedTextWriter** class, and lastly we create an instance of the **CodeGeneratorOptions** class to set output options for the generated file. You can see the content of the save file under the heading: The End Result earlier in this chapter.

```
Private void SaveCompileUnitToFile(CodeCompileUnit unit)
{
    var provider = new CSharpCodeProvider();
    var stream = new StreamWriter(dynamicPath +
        "program.cs");
    var textWriter = new IndentedTextWriter(stream);
    var options = new CodeGeneratorOptions();

    options.BlankLinesBetweenMembers = true;
    provider.GenerateCodeFromCompileUnit(unit,
        textWriter, options);
    textWriter.Close();
    stream.Close();
}
```

Compiling an Assembly from Source Code File

Once you have compiled one or more source code files, you can compile them into an assembly using one of the three available providers *Microsoft.CSharp.CSharpCodeProvider*, *Microsoft.VisualBasic.VBCode-Provider*, and *Microsoft.JavaScript.JScriptCodeProvider*.

The following sample code shows how you can build an executable assembly named *SampleApplication* from a .cs file named *Program.cs*.

First, we create an instance of the **CSharpCoodeProvider** class that will be used to compile the assembly, then we create an instance of the **CompilerParameters** class to add compiler settings such as which assemblies that are referenced by the assembly we are creating; if it is an executable we are creating; and the name of the finished assembly. Then we specify the path to the .cs file on the provider instance. The last thing we do is to return a **Boolean** stating if the creation was a success.

```
Private bool CompileToAssembly()
{
    var provider = new CSharpCodeProvider();

    var compilerSettings = new CompilerParameters();
    compilerSettings.ReferencedAssemblies.Add(
        "System.dll");
    compilerSettings.GenerateExecutable = true;
    compilerSettings.OutputAssembly = dynamicPath +
        "SampleApplication.exe";

    var compilationResults =
        provider.CompileAssemblyFromFile(
        compilerSettings, dynamicPath + "program.cs");

    return compilationResults.Errors.Count == 0;
}
```

Additional reading: "Generating and Compiling Source Code from a CodeDOM Graph"

Assemblies and the GAC

Two things you want to do before deploying an assembly to the users are to version and sign it; you also need to determine where the assembly should be deployed or installed: is it a stand-alone assembly such as a *Portable Executable (PE)* file or *Dynamic Link Library (DLL)*, or should it be installed in the *Global Assembly Cache (GAC)*?

An assembly does not have to consist of only one file; it can be made up of several files such as resource files and image files. You can look at an assembly as a building block for a .NET Framework application; an application can consist of several assemblies.

The assembly contains types and resources that form a unit of functionality. When compiling an assembly, the compiler creates *Intermediate Language (IL)* code that the *Just-In-Time (JIT)* compiler converts into machine code that the processor uses when the application runs. You can add assembly metadata to the assembly manifest and include images as resources in an assembly; the manifest contains information such as version, description and title of the assembly. Type metadata is added for the classes, interfaces and members to provide information about them.

The manifest data is used by the run-time to resolve references through the links to other files that are specified. The manifest is usually stored in one of the PE files, but can be stored in a separate file.

When you arrange the application into assemblies, you effectively create boundaries that make it possible to configure the usage of the content between different assemblies.

Boundaries

There are three assembly boundaries. The first is the ***Security boundary*** that is used to request permissions on assembly level, for instance I/O permissions for the assembly to write to disk. The permissions are added to the *security policy* at run-time to determine if access will be granted. The second boundary is the T***ype boundary,*** which makes it possible for two types to have the same name in different assemblies that are referenced without conflict because the assembly name is part of the type identity. The third boundary is the ***Eeference scope boundary*** The assembly manifest is used to resolve type and resource requests because it specifies what is exposed outside the assembly (private, public, internal, etc.)

Benefits

The benefits of using assemblies are that they are s***ingle units of deployment,*** which means that applications load assemblies when needed, providing a minimal download strategy where appropriate. ***Versioning*** can be implemented for *strong named assemblies,* making it easier to transition from one version of an assembly to another.

Additional reading: "Assemblies in the Common Language Runtime"

What is the GAC?

The default when building an assembly is that it is intended to be private for single application usage; if you want to reference an assembly from many applications, you can install it in the *Global Assembly Cache (GAC).* Any assembly that is meant to be installed in the *GAC* must have a *strong name*.

An integrity check is made of all the files that belong to the assembly before it can be installed in the *GAC*; this is to ensure that no tampering has been done to the assembly.

A ***strong name*** is a unique name that is comprised of the assembly name, version number, culture and a digital signature that has a public and private key.

You can find out which assemblies that currently are installed in the GAC by navigating to the *C:\Windows\assembly* folder for .NET versions older than 4.0 and *C:\Windows\Microsoft.NET\assembly\GAC_MSIL* for .NET versions 4.0 and newer. There you can find the following information about the assemblies: The assembly name, version number, culture (if applicable), public key token of the strong name, the assembly type and the processor architecture.

Assembly Name	Version	Cul...	Public Key Token	Processor Architecture
Accessibility	2.0.0.0		b03f5f7f11d50a3a	MSIL
ADODB	7.0.330...		b03f5f7f11d50a3a	
AspNetMMCExt	2.0.0.0		b03f5f7f11d50a3a	MSIL
ComSvcConfig	3.0.0.0		b03f5f7f11d50a3a	MSIL
Microsoft.Build.Engi...	2.0.0.0		b03f5f7f11d50a3a	MSIL
Microsoft.Build.Fra...	3.5.0.0		b03f5f7f11d50a3a	MSIL

Benefits

The benefits to installing strong named assemblies in the *GAC* are: ***Side-by-side deployment and execution*** which make it possible to have several versions of the same assembly installed simultaneously that can be targeted by different applications; ***Improved loading time*** because the assemblies installed in the *GAC* already have been validated on installation, they load faster than assemblies outside the *GAC;* ***Reduced memory consumption*** which means that only one instance of the assembly is loaded into memory and is shared between all applications that reference it; ***Improved search time*** because the CLR checks the *GAC* for strong named assemblies before looking in directories; and i***mproved maintainability*** which means when a change is made to the assembly, it will impact all the applications that uses it; you only have to make changes in one place.

Versioning

Versioning assemblies is very important to make it possible to track and reproduce production issues. A new assembly will be given a version number typically 1.0.0.0 by Visual Studio; it is the developer's responsibility to change the version number when new releases are delivered.

The version number consists of the following four segments: *<major version>.<minor version>.<build number>.<revision>*. You add or change the version number in the *AssemblyInfo.cs* file. The CLR uses the version number and other configuration information when loading an assembly.

Binding Redirect

By default, an application will run only with an assembly that has the correct version number; you can, however, override this by adding a version policy in the *application configuration file*, the *publisher policy file* or the computer's *administrator configuration* file.

To change the assembly a client application uses without deploying the client again, you can add a **<bindingRedirect>** element to one of the configuration files mentioned earlier. The **oldVersion** attribute specifies the version or range of versions you want to redirect from and the **newVersion** attribute specifies the new version that the client(s) should use.

The following sample shows how to redirect the versions between 1.1.0.0 and 1.4.0.0 to the version 2.0.0.0 in the *App.Config* file.

```
<configuration>
    <runtime>
        <assemblyBinding xmlns=
            "urn:schemas-microsoft-com:asm.v1">
            <dependentAssembly>
                <assemblyIdentity name="School"
                    publicKeyToken="32ab4ba45e0a69a1"
                    culture="en-us" />
                <bindingRedirect oldVersion="1.0.0.0"
                    newVersion="2.0.0.0"/>
```

```
            </dependentAssembly>
        </assemblyBinding>
    </runtime>
</configuration>
```

Additional reading: "Assembly Versioning"

Signing

To avoid manipulation and malicious code overwriting of your assemblies, they can be signed using a strong name that makes them globaly unique. Having a strong name public key you can use the functionality of the assembly, but you need the private key to make changes to the assembly.

A strong name needs a cryptographic *keypair* consisting of one public and one private key. The keypair is used when building the assembly to create the strong name. The strong name is comprised of the following information: the assembly name, version number, culture (if applicable), public key token and a digital signature.

Creating Keypairs

To generate a keypair file using the *Strong Name* tool (sn.exe), you open a *Visual Studio 2012 Command Prompt* window and use the **-k** switch with the sn.exe tool to generate a new file.

This command will generate a new key file with the name *SchoolKeyFile .snk*.

```
sn -k SchoolKeyFile.snk
```

You can also create a key file by opening the *project properties* window, checking the *Sign the assembly* checkbox and select **New** in the *Choose a strong name key file* combo box. Fill in the necessary fields and click **OK** to add the key file to the project.

Signing an Assembly

To assign a keyfile to an assembly, go to the *project properties* **Signing** tab, check the *Sign the assembly* checkbox and enter the name of the key file in the *Choose a strong name key file* combo box.

To sign an assembly, you add the code below in the *AssemblyInfo.cs* window.

```
[assembly: AssemblyKeyFileAttribute("SchoolKeyFile.snk")]
```

Delay Signing

Because the private key is sensitive information, you might not have access to it. You can then skip adding a strong name key file when signing an assembly and check the *Delay sign only* checkbox in the *project properties* **Signing** tab; this leaves space in the PE file to add the private key later using the sn.exe tool.

A project that has delayed signing activated cannot be run or debugged. When developing, you can however use the **-Vr** switch with the sn.exe tool to skip verification of the assembly.

The following command turns off the verification of the *School.dll* assembly.

```
sn -Vr School.dll
```

To sign an assembly with delayed signing activated, use the **-R** switch with the sn.exe tool.

The following command signs the *School.dll* that has delayed signing activated.

```
sn -R School.dll SchoolKeyFile.snk
```

Additional reading: "Delay Signing an Assembly"

Installing

You can add strong named assemblies to the GAC using either the *Global Asembly Cache tool* (Gacutil.exe) or *Windows Installer 2.0* (preferred method). The Gacutil.exe tool also can be used for development purposes to view the content of the GAC.

To install an assembly in the GAC, open a *Visual Studio 2012 Command Prompt* window and execute the following command.

```
gacutil /i "<path to assembly>"
```

You can inspect an assembly in the GAC by opening a *Visual Studio 2012 Command Prompt* window and executing the following command.

```
gacutil /l "<assembly name>"
```

Additional reading: "Global Assembly Cache"

Encrypting and Decrypting Data

Encrypting data is a way to keep it secure; we will have look at how to encrypt and decrypt data using symmetric and asymmetric encryption algorithms and hashing to create mathematical representations of your data. We also will look at how to use a X509 certificate when encrypting data.

Symmetric encryption

When implementing symmetric encryption, the same key is used for both encryption and decryption; it is therefore paramount that the key remains secret. Many symmetric algorithms use an *Initialization Vector (IV)* to randomize the first block of data; this makes it much more difficult to maliciously decrypt the data.

Some of the advantages with this type of encryption are that there is no limit on the amount of data that can be encrypted and symmetric algorithms are fast and use fewer system resources than asymmetric encryption.

Some disadvantages with this type of encryption are that the key can be comprised more easily because the same key is used for both encryption and decryption. This could lead to many different keys being used.

You find encryption classes in the **System.Security.Cryptography** namespace. All symmetric encryption classes derive from the abstract **SystemAlgorithm** class. All the symmetric encryption classes are block ciphers, which means that the cryptographic transformations are made on a block of a fixed length. The larger the key size, the more secure the encryption will be. The following table outlines the symmetric encryption classes that are available in the .NET Framework.

Algori-thm	.NET Framework class	Encryption Technique	Block Size	Key Size
DES	DESCryptoService-Provider	Bit shifting and bit substitution	64 bits	64 bits
AES	AesManaged	Substitution-Permutation Network (SPN)	128 bits	128, 192, or 256 bits
Rivest Cipher 2 (RC2)	RC2Crypto-ServiceProvider	Feistel network	64 bits	40-128 bits (increments of 8 bits)
Rijndael	RijndaelManaged	SPN	128-256 bits (increments of 32 bits)	128, 192, or 256 bits
Tripple-DES	TripleDES-CryptoService-Provider	Bit shifting and bit substitution	64 bits	128-192 bits

Additional reading: "SymmetricAlgorithm Class"

Encryption

When encrypting data using symmetric encryption, you usually create a secret key and an Initialization Vector (IV) from a salt and a password; the salt is used to make it more difficult perform malicious decrypting of the data. One of the classes that can be used to generate the secret key and IV is Rfc2898DeriveBytes. If you don't use a password and salt, you can obtain the secret key and IV from the cryptographic class you use for encryption, for instance, AesManaged.

The secret key and *IV* are then used when writing to the **CryptoStream** when encrypting the data and reading from the **CryptoStream** when decrypting the encrypted data.

Additional reading: "Rfc2898DeriveBytes Class" and "MSDN CryptoStream Class"

Example

The following sample code shows how you can use the **AesManaged** and **Rfc2898DeriveBytes** classes to encrypt a message.

Two properties with corresponding fields have been added to the class to hold the secret key and *IV* value; note that there are checks for the length of the field values and that an exception is thrown if no value is present.

In the constructor, we call one of the **GenerateKey** or the **GenerateKey-FromPasswordAndSalt** methods to generate the secret key and *IV* value. Note that only the **AesManaged** class is used in the first method and the **Rfc2898DeriveBytes** class is used in conjunction with the **Aes-Managed** class in the latter method.

In the **SymmetricEncryption** method that performs the encryption, we call the **CreateEncryptor** on an instance of the **AesManaged** class to create the encryptor that will use the secret key and *IV* to encrypt the message. We use a **MemoryStream** instance to store the encrypted bytes and a **CryptoStream** in conjunction with a **StreamWriter** to encrypt the bytes and write then to the **MemoryStream**. When the encryption has finished, we return the result as a **byte** array.

```
class Cryptography
{
    byte[] _secretKey;
    byte[] _secretInitializationVector;

    private byte[] SecretKey
    {
        get
        {
            if (_secretKey == null ||
                _secretKey.Length <= 0)
                throw new ArgumentNullException("Key");
            return _secretKey;
        }
        set { _secretKey = value; }
    }
    private byte[] SecretInitializationVector
    {
        get
        {
            if (_secretInitializationVector == null ||
                _secretInitializationVector.Length <= 0)
                throw new ArgumentNullException("Key");
            return _secretInitializationVector;
        }
        set { _secretInitializationVector = value; }
    }

    public Cryptography()
    {
        var password = "Pa$$w0rd";
        var salt = "S@lt";

        GenerateKey();
        //GenerateKeyFromPasswordAndSalt(password, salt);

        var encryptedText = SymmetricEncrpytion(
            "Jonas Fagerberg");
        var decryptedText =
            SymmetricDecryption(encryptedText);
    }
```

```
    private void GenerateKey()
    {
        using (AesManaged aesAlgorithm = new AesManaged())
        {
            SecretKey = aesAlgorithm.Key;
            SecretInitializationVector = aesAlgorithm.IV;
        }
    }

    private void GenerateKeyFromPasswordAndSalt(string
password, string salt)
    {
        using (var key = new Rfc2898DeriveBytes(password,
            Encoding.Unicode.GetBytes(salt)))
        {
            using (AesManaged aesAlgorithm = new
AesManaged())
            {
                SecretKey =
key.GetBytes(aesAlgorithm.KeySize / 8);
                SecretInitializationVector =
key.GetBytes(aesAlgorithm.BlockSize / 8);
            }
        }
    }

    private byte[] SymmetricEncrpytion(string
messageToEncrypt)
    {
        if (messageToEncrypt == null ||
messageToEncrypt.Length <= 0)
            throw new
ArgumentNullException("messageToEncrypt");

        byte[] encrypted = null;
```

```
        try
        {
            using (AesManaged aesAlgorithm =
            new AesManaged())
            {
                // Create a decryptor to perform
                // the stream transform.
                ICryptoTransform encryptor =
                    aesAlgorithm.CreateEncryptor(
                        SecretKey,
                        SecretInitializationVector);

                using (MemoryStream msEncrypt =
                new MemoryStream())
                {
                    using (CryptoStream csEncrypt =
                    new CryptoStream(msEncrypt,
                    encryptor, CryptoStreamMode.Write))
                    {
                        using (StreamWriter swEncrypt =
                        new StreamWriter(csEncrypt))
                        {
                            swEncrypt.Write(
                                messageToEncrypt);
                        }

                        encrypted = msEncrypt.ToArray();
                    }
                }
            }
        }
        catch (Exception ex) { }

        return encrypted;
    }
}
```

Decryption

In the **SymmetricDecryption** method that performs the decryption, we call the **CreateEncryptor** on an instance of the **AesManaged** class to create the decryptor that will use the secret key and IV to decrypt the message. We use a MemoryStream instance to hold the encrypted bytes and a **CryptoStream** in conjunction with a **StreamReader** to decrypt the bytes and convert them to a string using the **ReadToEnd** method on the **StreamReader**.

```
private string SymmetricDecryption(
byte[] messageToDecrypt)
{
    if (messageToDecrypt == null ||
        messageToDecrypt.Length <= 0)
            throw new ArgumentNullException(
                "messageToDecrypt");

    string plaintext = null;

    try
    {
        using (AesManaged aesAlg = new AesManaged())
        {
            // Create a decryptor to perform the
            // stream transform
            ICryptoTransform decryptor =
                aesAlg.CreateDecryptor(
                SecretKey, SecretInitializationVector);

            using (MemoryStream msDecrypt =
            new MemoryStream(messageToDecrypt))
            {
                using (CryptoStream csDecrypt =
                new CryptoStream(msDecrypt, decryptor,
                CryptoStreamMode.Read))
                {
                    using (StreamReader srDecrypt =
                    new StreamReader(csDecrypt))
                    {
                        plaintext = srDecrypt.ReadToEnd();
                    }
                }
            }
        }
    }
```

```
    catch (Exception ex) { }

    return plaintext;
}
```

Hashing

Hashing is very useful when you want the ability to check the integrity of a file (or other data); you can generate a numerical representation of the file data and use that to compare with a new hash of the file data before it is used. Hashes are considered safe when creating unique digital fingerprints.

The following table outlines some of the hash tables that .NET Framework provides.

Algorithm	.NET Framework class
SHA512-Managed	The **SHA512Managed** class is an implementation of the Secure Hash Algorithm (SHA) and is able to compute a 512-bit hash. The .NET Framework also includes classes that implement the SHA1, SHA256, and SHA384 algorithms.
HMACSHA512	The **HMACSHA512** class uses a combination of the SHA512 hash algorithm and the Hash-Based Message Authentication Code (HMAC) to compute a 512-bit hash.
MACTripleDES	The **MACTripleDES** class uses a combination of the TripleDES encryption algorithm and a Message Authentication Code (MAC) to compute a 64-bit hash.
MD5Crypto-ServiceProvider	The **MD5CryptoServiceProvider** class is an implementation of the Message Digest (MD) algorithm, which uses block chaining to compute a 128-bit hash.
RIPEMD160-Managed	The **RIPEMD160Managed** class is derived from the MD algorithm and is able to compute a 160-bit hash.

Generating a Hash

When generating a hash, we use an instance of the **HMACSHA512** class to generate the hash using the **ComputeHash** method; the result is returned as a **byte array**. In the following example, the two hashes should yield the same result because the same data are used to generate the hash.

```
class Cryptography
{
    public Cryptography()
    {
        byte[] dataToHash =
            Encoding.UTF8.GetBytes("Jonas");
        byte[] secretKey =
            Encoding.UTF8.GetBytes("Pa$$w0rd");

        var hash1 = ComputeHash(dataToHash, secretKey);
        var hash2 = ComputeHash(dataToHash, secretKey);
        var areEqual = Encoding.UTF8.GetString(hash1) ==
            Encoding.UTF8.GetString(hash2);
    }

    public byte[] ComputeHash(byte[] dataToHash,
    byte[] secretKey)
    {
        using (var hashAlgorithm =
        new HMACSHA512(secretKey))
        {
            using (var bufferStream =
            new MemoryStream(dataToHash))
            {
                return hashAlgorithm.ComputeHash(
                    bufferStream);
            }
        }
    }
}
```

Additional reading: "Hash Values Cryptographic Services"

Asymmetric encryption

When encrypting data with an asymmetric encryption algorithm, you use a public and private keypair that normally are mathematically linked. You can derive a public key from the private key, but not the other way around. The private key is never shared, the public key however is shared with any application that need to encrypt data; the private key is only used in applications that need to decrypt data.

Asymmetric encryption also can be used to sign data; you use the private key to sign the data and the public key to verify the data.

Two advantages with asymmetric encryption are that it is easier to determine which applications should use what key dependent on if the application is encrypting or decrypting data. Bruteforce attacks to crack the encryption is much harder because larger keys can be used than with symmetric encryption.

Two disadvantages with asymmetric encryption are that you can only encrypt small amounts of data and the size of the data that can be encrypted is proportional to the key size. Using a key of 1024 bits can only encrypt data with a size less than 128 bytes. Asymmetric algorithms are generally much slower than symmetric algorithms.

To use asymmetric encryption on larger amounts of data you could combine the usage of asymmetric encryption with symmetric.

The following steps are considered best practice when encrypting with asymmetric and symmetric algorithms together: use a symmetric encryption class such as AesManaged to encrypt the data then use an asymmetric algorithm to encrypt the symmetric key. When writing the data to the stream you write the following information: The length of the *IV*, the length of the encrypted secret key, the *IV*, the encrypted secret key, the encrypted data. When decrypting you simply read through the stream, extract the data, decrypt the data symmetric encryption key and decrypt the data.

You can use the **RSACryptoServiceProvider** to encrypt and sign data using the *RSA* algorithm (created by creators **R**ivest, **S**hamir, and **A**dleman). Using the default encryption provider, the key lengths can vary between 384 to 512 bits in 8-bit increments. Using the *Micrososft Enhanced Encryption Provider* the key size can be as large as 16,384 bits.

You can use the **DSACryptoServiceProvider** to sign data using the *Digital Signature Algorithm (DSA)* with key sizes from 512 to 1,024 bits in 64-bit increments.

Additional reading: "Public-Key Encryption C#"

Encrypting Data

The asymmetric encryption class **RSACryptoServiceProvider** is located in the **System.Security.Cryptography** namespace and provides members that make it possible to implement asymmetric encryption fully in applications. If you use the default constructor of the **RSACryptoServiceProvider** class then private and public keys will be generated automatically.

The following sample code shows how you can implement properties in a **struct** that generates and returns the private and public keys needed when using *RSA* encryption and decryption. Note that the properties check to see if keys already have been generated for the current instance of the **struct**. Also note that we send in false to the **ExportParameters** when generating the encryption key to only generate the public parameter values of the **RSAParameters** structure; passing in true when we want both the public and private parameter values.

```
struct RsaKeys
{
    private RSAParameters _RSAEncryptionKey;
    private RSAParameters _RSADecryptionKey;

    public RSAParameters RSAEncryptionKey
    {
        get
        {
            if (_RSAEncryptionKey.Exponent == null)
                GetRSAKey(); return _RSAEncryptionKey;
        }
    }
    public RSAParameters RSADecryptionKey
    {
        get
        {
            if (_RSADecryptionKey.Exponent == null)
                GetRSAKey(); return _RSADecryptionKey;
        }
    }
    private void GetRSAKey()
    {
        try
        {
            using (RSACryptoServiceProvider RSA =
            new RSACryptoServiceProvider())
            {
                _RSAEncryptionKey =
                    RSA.ExportParameters(false);
                _RSADecryptionKey =
                    RSA.ExportParameters(true);
            }
        }
        catch (CryptographicException e)
        {
            _RSAEncryptionKey = new RSAParameters();
            _RSADecryptionKey = new RSAParameters();
        }
    }
}
```

The following sample code shows how you can implement asymmetric encryption using the **RSACryptoServiceProvider** class. First, we use the **RSAKeys** struct previously described to generate the private and public keys, then we call the **AsymmetricEncryption** method to encrypt the data; in this method we start by converting the data string to a **byte** array that will be encrypted. We then use an instance of the **RSACryptoServiceProvider** class to perform the encryption using the Encrypt method. Note however that before we encrypt we import the key to the provider.

```
class Cryptography
{
   public Cryptography()
   {
       RsaKeys rsaKeys = new RsaKeys();
       var encryptedMessage = AsymmetricEncryption(
           "Jonas Fagerberg", rsaKeys.RSAEncryptionKey);
       var decryptedMessage = AsymmetricDecryption(
           encryptedMessage, rsaKeys.RSADecryptionKey);
   }

   private byte[] AsymmetricEncryption(
   string messageToEncrypt, RSAParameters key,
   bool useOaepPadding = true)
   {
       var messageBytes = Encoding.Default.GetBytes(
           messageToEncrypt);
       byte[] encryptedBytes = null;

       using (var rsaProvider =
       new RSACryptoServiceProvider())
       {
           rsaProvider.ImportParameters(key);
           encryptedBytes = rsaProvider.Encrypt(
               messageBytes, useOaepPadding);
       }
       return encryptedBytes;
   }
}
```

The **useOaepPadding** parameter determines if *Optimal Asymmetric Encryption Padding (OAEP)* should be used. If you set it to false, then *PKCS#1 v1*.5 padding will be used instead.

Decrypting Data

The following sample code shows how you can implement asymmetric encryption using the **RSACryptoServiceProvider** class. In this example, we pass in the byte array generated when encrypting the data on the previous row.In reality, you probably would read the data from a data storage of some kind or receive it as a parameter from a method call.

We use the key generated from the **RsaKeys** struct passing it in as a parameter to the **AsymmetricDecryption** method that decrypts the previously encrypted data in the **byte** array. We use an instance of the **RSACryptoServiceProvider** class to perform the decryption using the Decrypt method. Note however that before we decrypt the data, we import the key to the provider. Lastly, we convert the decrypted **byte** array to a **string**.

```
Class Cryptography
{
    public Cryptography()
    {
        RsaKeys rsaKeys = new RsaKeys();
        var encryptedMessage = AsymmetricEncryption(
            "Jonas Fagerberg", rsaKeys.RSAEncryptionKey);
        var decryptedMessage = AsymmetricDecryption(
            encryptedMessage, rsaKeys.RSADecryptionKey);
    }

    private string AsymmetricDecryption(
    byte[] messageToDecrypt, RSAParameters key,
    bool useOaepPadding = true)
    {
        var decryptedText = string.Empty;
```

```
        using (var rsaProvider =
        new RSACryptoServiceProvider())
        {
            rsaProvider.ImportParameters(key);
            var decryptedBytes = rsaProvider.Decrypt(
                messageToDecrypt, useOaepPadding);
            decryptedText = Encoding.Default.GetString(
                decryptedBytes);
        }

        return decryptedText;
    }
}
```

Additional reading: "RSACryptoServiceProvider.Encrypt Method" and "RSACryptoServiceProvider Class"

X509 Certificates

Another way of handling keys is to use a X509 certificate that is installed into the certificate store on the computer running the application. Apart from key information, a certificate contains information about the organization supplying the data. .NET Framework provides the necessary tools to generate and maintain X509 certificates.

Create a X509 Certificate

You create certificates by running the **MakeCert** application in a *Micrososft Visual Studio Command Prompt* window. There are a number of switches that can be used with the **MakeCert** tool.

Switch	Description
-n	Enables you to specify the name of the certificate.
-a	Enables you to specify the algorithm that the certificate uses.
-pe	Enables you to create a certificate that allows exporting of a private key.

Switch	Description
-r	Enables you to create a self-signed certificate.
-sr	Enables you to specify the name of the certificate store where the certificate will be imported.
-ss	Enables you to specify the name of the container within the certificate store where the certificate will be imported.
-sky	Enables you to specify the type of key that the certificate will contain.

The following sample command shows how you can use the **MakeCert** tool to generate a self-signed certificate that contains both a public and a private key.

```
makecert -n "CN=SchoolCertificate" -a sha1 -pe -r -sr
LocalMachine -ss my -sky exchange
```

Additional reading: "Makecert.exe (Certificate Creation Tool)"

You can manage your certificates using the *Microsoft Management Console Certificates Snap-in*; visit "MSDN Working with Certificates" for more information.

Encryption Keys and the X509 Certificate

You find the X509Store and X509Certificate2 classes, which are used when handling certificates, in the System.Security.Cryptography.X509-Certificates namespace. the X509Store class is used to access a certificate store and the **X509Certificate2** class is used to create an in-memory representation of a certificate; use this object to access information such as key values.

The following list describes some of the members of the **X509Certificate2** class.

- **HasPrivateKey**
  Shows if a certificate holds a private key.
- **FriendlyName**
  Shows a more descriptive name of the certificate.
- **GetPublicKeyString**
  Fetches the public key that is associated with the certificate.
- **PublicKey**
  Contains the public key as a **PublicKey** object.
- **PrivateKey**
  Contains the public key as a **AsymmetricAlgorithm** object.

The **PublicKey** and **PrivateKey** properties can be used to create an instance of the **RSACryptoServiceProvider** class.

Listing the certificates in a Certificate Store

The following sample code shows how you can list the names of all certificates in a certificate store.

```
Class Cryptography
{
    private void ListCertificates()
    {
        var store = new X509Store(StoreName.My,
            StoreLocation.LocalMachine);

        store.Open(OpenFlags.ReadOnly);
```

```
        foreach (var storeCertificate in
        store.Certificates)
            Console.WriteLine(String.Format(
                "Certificate: {0}",
                storeCertificate.SubjectName.Name));

        store.Close();
    }
}
```

Fetch a certificate from a Certificate Store

The following sample code shows how you can fetch certificate from a certificate store. Start by creating a **X509Store** instance that opens the desired certificate store; use the **Open** method to open the store passing in a flag stating what read and write privileges are to be used. Then you loop over the **Certificates** collection until you find the desired certificate and return it.

```
Class Cryptography
{
    private X509Certificate2 GetCertificate(
    string certificateName)
    {
        var store = new X509Store(StoreName.My,
            StoreLocation.LocalMachine);
        var certificate = default(X509Certificate2);
        var name = String.Format("CN={0}",
            certificateName);

        store.Open(OpenFlags.ReadOnly);

        foreach (var storeCertificate in
        store.Certificates)
        {
            if (storeCertificate.SubjectName.Name == name)
            {
                certificate = storeCertificate;
                continue;
            }
        }
```

```
        store.Close();

        return certificate;
    }
}
```

Encrypting Using a X509 Certificate Key

First, we fetch the certificate from the certificate store using the previously described **GetCertificate** method; then we call the **AsymmetricX509Encryption** method to encrypt the data passing in the certificate as a parameter. In the method we then covert the string to a **byte** array that is encrypted using the **Encrypt** method of the **RSACryptoServiceProvider** instance that we created using the passed-in certificates' **PublicKey.Key** property that contains an **AsymmetricAlgorithm** object.

```
Class Cryptography
{
    public Cryptography()
    {
        var certificate =
            GetCertificate("SchoolCertificate");
        var encryptedX509Message =
            AsymmetricX509Encryption(
                "Jonas Fagerberg", certificate);
        var decryptedX509Message =
            AsymmetricX509Decryption(
                encryptedX509Message, certificate);
    }

    private byte[] AsymmetricX509Encryption(
    string messageToEncrypt, X509Certificate2
    certificate, bool useOaepPadding = true)
    {
        var messageBytes = Encoding.Default.GetBytes(
            messageToEncrypt);
        byte[] encryptedBytes = null;
```

```
        using (var rsaProvider =
        (RSACryptoServiceProvider)certificate
        .PublicKey.Key)
            encryptedBytes = rsaProvider.Encrypt(
                messageBytes, useOaepPadding);

        return encryptedBytes;
    }
}
```

Decrypting Using a X509 Certificate Key

First, we fetch the certificate from the certificate store using the previously described **GetCertificate** method; then we call the **AsymmetricX509Decryption** method to decrypt the data passing in the certificate as a parameter. In the method, we then call the **Decrypt** method of the **RSACryptoServiceProvider** instance that we created using the passed-in certificates' **PrivateKey** property that contains an **AsymmetricAlgorithm** object. Lastly, we covert the decrypted **byte** array to a **string** that is returned.

```
Class Cryptography
{
    public Cryptography()
    {
        var certificate = GetCertificate(
            "SchoolCertificate");
        var encryptedX509Message =
            AsymmetricX509Encryption(
                "Jonas Fagerberg", certificate);
        var decryptedX509Message =
            AsymmetricX509Decryption(
                encryptedX509Message, certificate);
    }
```

```
    private string AsymmetricX509Decryption(
    byte[] messageToDecrypt, X509Certificate2
    certificate, bool useOaepPadding = true)
    {
        var decryptedText = string.Empty;
        using (var rsaProvider =
        (RSACryptoServiceProvider)certificate.PrivateKey)
        {
            var decryptedBytes = rsaProvider.Decrypt(
                messageToDecrypt, useOaepPadding);
            decryptedText = Encoding.Default.GetString(
                decryptedBytes);
        }

        return decryptedText;
    }
}
```

IMAGES

CPSIA information can be obtained at www.ICGtesting.com
Printed in the USA
LVOW10s1529070415

433608LV00002B/388/P

9 781494 208394